R. Gupta's®

Arunachal Pradesh

GENERAL KNOWLEDGE

A complete description of History, Geography, Economy, Polity, Flora & Fauna, Culture and more.

Compiled & Edited by

SANJAY KUMAR
RPH EDITORIAL BOARD

2020 EDITION

Ramesh Publishing House, NEW DELHI

Published by:

O.P. Gupta *for* Ramesh Publishing House

Admin. Office:

12-H, New Daryaganj Road, Opp. Officers' Mess,
New Delhi-110002 ✆ 23261567, 23275224, 23275124

E-mail: info@rameshpublishinghouse.com
Website: www.rameshpublishinghouse.com

Showroom:

● Balaji Market, Nai Sarak, Delhi-6 ✆ 23253720, 23282525
● 4457, Nai Sarak, Delhi-6, ✆ 23918938

Book Code: R-1067

ISBN: 978-81-7812-717-0

HSN Code: 49011010

CONTENTS

WHO'S WHO*

Governor : B.D. Mishra
Chief Minister : Pema Khandu

Pema Khandu

MINISTERS

Sl.No.	Name	Portfolio(s)
1.	Pema Khandu	C.M., All Departments not assigned to Deputy Chief Minister and any Cabinet Minister.
2.	Chowna Mein	Deputy Chief Minister, Finance and Investment, Power and Non Conventional Energy Resources
3.	Wangki Lowang	PHE & Water Supply, Deptt. of Tirap, Changlang & Longding
4.	Honchun Ngandam	Rural Works
5.	Kamlung Mossang	Urban Development, Municipal Admn. & Govt. Estates, Civil Supplies & Consumer Affairs.
6.	Alo Libang	Health & Family Welfare, Social Welfare, Women & Child Development, Social Justice, Empowerment & Tribal Affairs
7.	Bamang Felix	Home and Inter State Border Affairs, Rural Development and Panchayati Raj, Parliamentary Affairs
8.	Tumke Bagra	Industries, Skill Development, Textile & Handicrafts, Trade & Commerce
9.	Mama Natung	Youth Affairs and Sports, Water Resources
10.	Tage Taki	Agriculture, Horticulture, Animal Husbandary & Veterinary, Dairy Development, Fisheries
11.	Taba Tedir	Education, Cultural Affairs, Department of Indigeneous Affairs
12.	Nakap Nalo	Tourism, Transport and Civil Aviation

*As on December 03, 2019.

REPRESENTATION OF STATE IN LOK SABHA

Kiren Rijiju (BJP)
West Parliamentary Constituency

Tapir Gao (BJP)
East Parliamentary Constituency

REPRESENTATION OF STATE IN RAJYA SABHA
Mukut Mithi (INC)

MEMBERS OF LEGISLATIVE ASSEMBLY
(ELECTION-2019)

S.No.	Constituency	Name of Member
1.	Lumla	Jambey Tashi
2.	Tawang	Tsering Tashi
3.	Mukto	Pema Khandu
4.	Dirang	Phurpatsering
5.	Kalaktang	Dorjee Wangdi Kharma
6.	Thrizino-Buragaon	Kumsi Sidisow
7.	Bomdila	Dongru Siongju
8.	Bameng	Goruk Pordung
9.	Chayangtajo	Hayeng Mangfi
10.	Seppa East	Tapuk Taku
11.	Seppa West	Mama Natung
12.	Pakke-Kessang	Biyuram Wahge
13.	Itanagar	Techi Kaso
14.	Dcimukh	Tana Halt Tara
15.	Sagalee	Nabam Tuki
16.	Yachuli	Taba Tedir
17.	Ziro-Hapou	Tage Taki
18.	Palin	Balo Raja
19.	Nyapin	Bamang Felix
20.	Tali	Jikke Tako
21.	Koloriang	Lokam Tassar
22.	Nacho	Nakap Nalo

S.No.	Constituency	Name of Member
23.	Taliha	Nyato Rigia
24.	Daporijo	Tani Ya Soki
25.	Raga	Tarin Dakpe
26.	Damporijo	Rode Bui
27.	Liromoba	Nyamar Karbak
28.	Lkabali	Kardo Nyigyor
29.	Basar	Gokar Basar
30.	Along West	Tumke Bagra
31.	Along East	Kento Jini
32.	Rumgong	Talem Taboh
33.	Mechuka	Pasang Dorjee Sona
34.	Tuting-Yingkiong	Alo Libang
35.	Pangin	Ojing Tasing
36.	Nari-Koyu	Kento Rina
37.	Pasighat West	Ninong Ering
38.	Pasighat East	Kaling Moyong
39.	Mebo	Lombo Tayeng
40.	Mariyang-Geku	Kanggong Taku
41.	Anini	Mopi Mihu
42.	Dambuk	Gum Tayeng
43.	Roing	Mutchu Mithi
44.	Tezu	Karikho Kri
45.	Hayuliang	Dasanglu Pul
46.	Chowkham	Chowna Mein
47.	Namsai	Chau Zingnu Namchoom
48.	Lekang	Jummum Ete Deori
49.	Bordumsa-Diyum	Somlung Mossang
50.	Miao	Kamlung Mossang
51.	Nampong	Laisam Simai
52.	Changlang South	Phosum Khimhun
53.	Changlang North	Tesam Pongte
54.	Namsang	Wangki Lowang
55.	Khonsa East	Wanglam Sawin
56.	Khonsa West	Chakat Aboh
57.	Borduriabogapani	Wanglin Lowangdong
58.	Kanubari	Gabriel Denwang Wangsu
59.	Longding-Pumao	Tanpho Wangnaw
60.	Pongchau-Wakka	Honchun Ngandam

GOVERNORS OF ARUNACHAL PRADESH

S.No.	Name	From	To
1.	Bhisma Narain Singh	20-02-1987	18-03-1987
2.	R.D. Pradhan	19-03-1987	16-03-1990
3.	Dr. Gopal Singh	17-03-1990	08-05-1990
4.	D.D. Thakur	09-05-1990	16-03-1991
5.	Loknath Mishra	17-03-1991	25-03-1991
6.	S.N. Dwivedy	26-03-1991	04-07-1993
7.	Madhukar Dighe	05-07-1993	20-10-1993
8.	Mata Prasad	21-10-1993	16-05-1999
9.	Lt. General (Rtd.) S.K. Sinha, PVSM	17-05-1999	01-08-1999
10.	Arvind Dave	02-08-1999	12-06-2003
11.	V.C. Pande	13-06-2003	15-12-2004
12.	S.K. Singh	16-12-2004	23-01-2007
13.	M.M. Jacob (Acting)	24-01-2007	06-04-2007
14.	K. Sankaranarayanan (Acting)	07-04-2007	14-04-2007
15.	S.K. Singh	15-04-2007	03-09-2007
16.	K. Sankaranarayanan (Acting)	04-09-2007	26-01-2008
17.	General (Rtd.) J.J. Singh	27-01-2008	28-05-2013
18.	Lt. General (Rtd.) Nirbhay Sharma	28-05-2013	12-05-2015
19.	Jyoti Prasad Rajkhowa	12-05-2015	14-09-2016
20.	V. Shanmuganathan (Add. Ch.)	14-09-2016	27-01-2017
20.	P. Balakrishna Acharya (Add. Ch.)	28-1-2017	03-10-2017
21.	B.D. Mishra	03-10-2017	— — —

CHIEF MINISTERS OF ARUNACHAL PRADESH

S.No.	Name	From	To
1.	P.K. Thungon	13-08-1975	18-09-1979
2.	Tomo Riba	18-09-1979	03-11-1979
3.	Gegong Apang	18-01-1980	19-01-1999
4.	Mukut Mithi	19-01-1999	03-08-2003
5.	Gegong Apang	03-08-2003	09-04-2007
6.	Dorjee Khandu	09-04-2007	30-04-2011
7.	Jarbom Gamlin	05-05-2011	01-11-2011
8.	Nabam Tuki	01-11-2011	26-01-2016
9.	Kalikho Pul	19-02-2016	13-07-2016
10.	Nabam Tuki	13-07-2016	17-07-2016
11.	Pema Khandu	17-07-2016	— — —

GOVERNMENT OF INDIA

✧ **President :** Ram Nath Kovind

✧ **Vice President :** M. Venkaiah Naidu

THE UNION COUNCIL OF MINISTERS*

CABINET MINISTERS

✦ **Narendra Modi**	: Prime Minister and also in-charge of: Ministry of Personnel, Public Grievances and Pensions; Department of Atomic Energy; Department of Space; and All important policy issues; and All other portfolios not allocated to any Minister.
✦ **Amit Shah**	: Home Affairs
✦ **Rajnath Singh**	: Defence
✦ **Nirmala Sitharaman**	: Finance; and Corporate Affairs
✦ **Nitin Gadkari**	: Road Transport and Highways; and Micro, Small and Medium Enterprises
✦ **D.V. Sadananda Gowda**	: Chemicals and Fertilizers
✦ **Ram Vilas Paswan**	: Consumer Affairs, Food and Public Distribution
✦ **Narendra Singh Tomar**	: Agriculture and Farmers Welfare; Rural Development; and Panchayati Raj
✦ **Ravi Shankar Prasad**	: Law and Justice; Communications; and Electronics and Information Technology
✦ **Harsimrat Kaur Badal**	: Food Processing Industries
✦ **Thawar Chand Gehlot**	: Social Justice and Empowerment
✦ **Subrahmanyam Jaishankar**	: External Affairs
✦ **Ramesh Pokhriyal Nishank**	: Human Resource Development
✦ **Arjun Munda**	: Tribal Affairs

*As on December 03, 2019.

✦ **Smriti Irani**	: Women and Child Development; and Textiles.
✦ **Dr Harshavardhan**	: Health and Family Welfare; Science and Technology; and Earth Sciences
✦ **Prakash Javadekar**	: Environment, Forest and Climate Change; and Information and Broadcasting minister, Additional Charge—Heavy Industries and Public Enterprise
✦ **Piyush Goyal**	: Railways; and Commerce and Industry
✦ **Dharmendra Pradhan**	: Petroleum and Natural Gas; and Steel.
✦ **Mukhtar Abbas Naqvi**	: Minority Affairs
✦ **Prahlad Joshi**	: Parliamentary Affairs; Coal; and Mines
✦ **Mahendra Nath Pandey**	: Skill Development and Entrepreneurship
✦ **Giriraj Singh**	: Animal Husbandry, Dairying and Fisheries
✦ **Gajendra Singh Shekhawat**	: Jal Shakti

MINISTERS OF STATE (INDEPENDENT CHARGES)

✦ **Santosh Gangwar**	: Labour and Employment
✦ **Rao Inderjit Singh**	: Statistics and Programme Implementation; and Planning.
✦ **Shripad Yesso Naik**	: Ayurveda, Yoga and Naturopathy, Unani, Siddha and Homoeopathy (AYUSH) (Ind. Ch.); Defence.
✦ **Jitendra Singh**	: Development of North Eastern Region (Ind. Ch.); Personnel, Public Grievances and Pensions, Atomic Energy, Department of Space, Prime Minister Office.
✦ **Kiren Rijiju**	: Youth Affairs and Sports (Ind. Ch.); Minority Affairs.
✦ **Prahlad Singh Patel**	: Culture; and Tourism
✦ **Raj Kumar Singh**	: Power; New and Renewable Energy (Ind. Ch.); Skill Development and Entrepreneurship.
✦ **Hardeep Singh Puri**	: Housing and Urban Affairs; Civil Aviation (Ind. Ch.); Commerce and Industry.
✦ **Mansukh Mandaviya**	: Shipping (Ind. Ch.); Chemicals and Fertilizers.

MINISTERS OF STATE

✦ **Faggan Singh Kulaste**	:	Steel
✦ **Ashwini Kumar Chaubey**	:	Health and Family Welfare.
✦ **Arjun Ram Meghwal**	:	Parliamentary Affairs; and Heavy Industries and Public Enterprises
✦ **General (Retd) VK Singh**	:	Road Transport and Highways
✦ **Krishan Pal Gurjar**	:	Social Justice and Empowerment
✦ **Raosaheb Dadarao Danve**	:	Consumer Affairs, Food and Public Distribution
✦ **Gangapuram Kishan Reddy**	:	Home Affairs
✦ **Purshottam Rupala**	:	Agriculture and Farmers Welfare
✦ **Ramdas Athawale**	:	Social Justice and Empowerment
✦ **Sadhvi Niranjan Jyoti**	:	Rural Development
✦ **Babul Supriyo**	:	Environment, Forest and Climate Change
✦ **Sanjeev Kumar Balyan**	:	Animal Husbandry, Dairying and Fisheries
✦ **Sanjay Shamrao Dhotre**	:	Human Resource Development; Communications; and Electronics and Information Technology.
✦ **Anurag Thakur**	:	Finance; and Corporate Affairs
✦ **Suresh Channabasappa Angadi**	:	Railways
✦ **Nityanand Rai**	:	Home Affairs
✦ **Rattan Lal Kataria**	:	Jal Shakti; and Social Justice and Empowerment
✦ **V Muraleedharan**	:	External Affairs; and Parliamentary Affairs
✦ **Renuka Singh Saruta**	:	Tribal Affairs
✦ **Som Parkash**	:	Commerce and Industry
✦ **Rameswar Teli**	:	Food Processing Industries
✦ **Pratap Chandra Sarangi**	:	Micro, Small and Medium Enterprises; and Animal Husbandry, Dairying and Fisheries
✦ **Kailash Choudhary**	:	Agriculture and Farmers Welfare.
✦ **Debasree Chaudhuri**	:	Women and Child Development

GOVERNORS AND CHIEF MINISTERS OF STATES

States	Governor	Chief Minister
Andhra Pradesh	Biswa Bhusan Harichandan	Y.S. Jaganmohan Reddy
Arunachal Pradesh	B.D. Mishra	Pema Khandu
Assam	Jagdish Mukhi	Sarbananda Sonowal
Bihar	Phagu Chauhan	Nitish Kumar
Chattisgarh	Anysuya Uikey	Bhupesh Baghel
Goa	Satyapal Malik	Pramod Sawant
Gujarat	Acharya Dev Vrat	Vijay Rupani
Haryana	Satyadev Narayan Arya	Manohar Lal Khattar
Himachal Pradesh	Bandaru Dattatraya	Jairam Thakur
Jharkhand	Draupadi Murmu	Raghuvar Das
Karnataka	Vajubhai Vala	B.S. Yediyurappa
Kerala	Arif Mohammed Khan	Pinarayi Vijayan
Madhya Pradesh	Lalji Tandon	Kamal Nath
Maharashtra	Bhagat Singh Koshyari	Uddhav Thackeray
Manipur	Najma Heptulla	N. Biren Singh
Meghalaya	Tathagata Roy	Conrad K. Sangma
Mizoram	P.S. Shridharan Pillai	Zoramthanga
Nagaland	R.N. Ravi	Neiphiu Rio
Odisha	Prof. Ganeshi Lal	Navin Patnayak
Punjab	V.P. Singh Badnore	Capt. Amarinder Singh
Rajasthan	Kalraj Mishra	Ashok Gehlot
Sikkim	Ganga Prasad	Prem Singh Tamang
Tamil Nadu	Banwari Lal Purohit	E.K. Palaniswami
Telangana	Dr. T. Soundararajan	K. Chandrasekhar Rao
Tripura	Ramesh Bais	Biplab Kumar Deb
Uttarakhand	Baby Rani Maurya	Trivendra Singh Rawat
Uttar Pradesh	Anandiben Patel	Yogi Adityanath
West Bengal	Jagdeep Dhankhar	Mamata Banerjee

CAPITALS, LT. GOVERNORS/ADMINISTRATORS AND CHIEF MINISTERS OF UNION TERRITORIES

Territory	Capitals	Lt. Governors/Administrators	Chief Minister
Andaman & Nicobar Islands	Port Blair	Devendra Kumar Joshi	...
Chandigarh	Chandigarh	V.P. Singh Badnore	...
Dadra & Nagar Haveli	Silvassa	Praful Khoda Patel	...
Delhi	Delhi	Anil Baijal	Arvind Kejriwal
Diu and Daman	Daman	Praful Khoda Patel	...
Lakshadweep	Kavaratti	Dineshwar Sharma	...
Puducherry	Puducherry	Kiran Bedi	V. Narayanasamy
Jammu & Kashmir	Srinagar (Summer) Jammu (Winter)	Girish Chandra Murmu	...
Ladakh	Leh	R.K. Mathur	...

CURRENT AFFAIRS

Budget 2019-20

Arunachal Pradesh Deputy Chief Minister Chowna Mein, who also holds the Finance portfolio, presented the maiden Budget-2019-20 of the Pema Khandu-led BJP Government in the state on July 9, 2019. Presenting the ₹ 520.98 crore deficit budget for the 2019-20 fiscal, the Deputy Chief Minister said the revenue receipts of ₹ 20857.92 crore and capital receipts of ₹ 1535.53 crore has been projected making the total receipts of ₹ 22393.45 crore as against the total receipts of ₹ 21301.83 crore in Revised Estimates of 2018-19. State share of Central taxes has been pegged at a level of ₹ 11,571 crore as per the Union budget 2019-20 and the projected State's own tax revenue at a level of ₹ 1440 crore. The non-tax revenue projection for 2019-20 has been pegged at ₹ 1050 crore. Highlighting the state government's achievements in last two and half years of its first stint under the leadership of Chief Minister Pema Khandu, Mr Mein said several innovative policy and governance reforms have been undertaken for ensuring transparency, increasing overall efficiency, removing red-tapeism and corrupt practices in the functioning of all the departments of the Government. "Now our Government aspires to become the 'most developed' and 'happiest state' in India," he said, adding "One of the most striking features of this year's budget is alignment of our schemes with Sustainable Development Goals (SDGs)". Stating that economy of the frontier state is primarily based on agriculture and allied activities, Mein said, State Government is working on a mission mode to achieve the vision of Prime Minister Narendra Modi for doubling farmers' income by 2022. Revamping agriculture and allied sector is a key to achieve food security, improved nutrition and promote sustainable livelihood in our state, he added. Proposing to expand the coverage of the Chief Minister's Sashakt Kisan Yojana to include various horticulture crops, the FM said a fund provision of ₹ 95.70 crore is proposed to be allocated for the said scheme. The Budget also proposed to set up Research and Development (R&D) Center for kiwi at Ziro in Lower Subansiri district and R&D Center for orange at Roing in Lower Dibang Valley district allocating ₹ 2 crore each.

Tawang Festival 2019

Organized by Arunachal Pradesh Tourism Department, Tawang Festival was held from 28 to 31, October 2019. US (United States) Ambassador to India,

Kenneth Ian Juster inaugurated the festival in presence of Chief Minister Pema Khandu. The name Tawang came to the festival after the name of a hill station Tawang in Arunachal Pradesh. The purpose of celebrating the festival is not only to make tourists coming from abroad, but also aware of the beauty, tradition, and culture of Arunachal Pradesh. Buddhist traditions and their different lifestyles can also be experienced by attending this festival. The most special attractions of the Tawang Festival were 'Yak Dance', Aji-Lhamu dance, tribal participation with various traditional rituals, street performances.

Journalist Taro Chatung Passes Away

On October 26, 2019, renowned journalist Taro Chatung, considered as a pioneer of electronic media in Arunachal Pradesh, has passed away at a hospital in Itanagar after a prolonged illness. He was 57. He hailed from Kudumbarang, Hija, in Lower Subansiri district, Arunachal Pradesh. Chatung is best known for his straight questions in Doordarshan's (DD) 'News and Views' program, which broke all viewership records. He is also called the 'father of electronic media' in the state. In 1988, He started on his journalism & filmmaking career after leaving his state civil service job. He was a founding member of the Arunachal Press Club (APC) and Arunachal Pradesh Union of Working Journalists (APUWJ). He worked as the president of both the union and the club. Chatung, a state gold medal awardee, was one of the first in the state to direct and produce a Hindi feature film as it is spoken in Arunachal Pradesh.

Dikshi Hydroelectric Project Inaugurated

On September 14, 2019, The Chief Minister of Arunachal Pradesh Pema Khandu has inaugurated the 24 kW(Kilowatt) Dikshi Hydroelectric Project on the Phudungto river at Dikshi village in West Kameng district of Arunachal Pradesh. The project was developed by a Hyderabad (Telangana) based firm Devi Energies Private Limited. It is State's first community-managed mini-hydro electric project and also the first independent power project of its kind in the Northeast. The power plant is expected to generate 112.40 gigawatt-hours of electricity for addressing the power requirements of East and West Kameng districts besides major defence establishments. The plant consists 3 Francis type turbo-generators having capacity of 8.0 MW each, was completed in a record time of 4 years since commencement in 2016 with an investment amount of about 430 crore rupees. The Arunachal State government will get 10% as free power from the 2nd year of the plant's operation.

Assembly Election-2019

BJP leader Pema Khandu on May 29, 2019 took oath as the chief minister of Arunachal Pradesh. Eleven Cabinet ministers, including Chowna Mein, were also administered the oath. Mr. Mein took oath as the deputy chief minister, while 10 others—Honchun Ngandam, Wangki Lowang, Alo Libang, Kamlung Mossang, Bamang Felix, Tumke Bagra, Mama Natung, Nakap Nalo, Tage Taki and Taba Tedir—were sworn in as ministers. The oath of office and secrecy was administered by A.P's Governor Brigadier (Retd.) B.D. Mishra. For the first time formal installation ceremony was held in Itanagar's landmark convention centre, named after his father Dorjee Khandu instead of Raj Bhavan where his predecessors were sworn in. The ceremony was attended by chief ministers of five north-eastern States namely, Assam, Nagaland, Manipur, Tripura

SEAT TALLY	
Party	**Won**
Bharatiya Janata Party	41
Independent	2
Indian National Congress	4
Janata Dal (United)	7
National People's Party	5
People's Party of Arunachal	1
Total	**60**

and Meghalaya. Pema Khandu pitchforked into politics after the death of his father in a helicopter crash in April 2011. His father, Dorjee Khandu was the fifth CM of Arunachal Pradesh. After his father's death he was made the State's Water Resources Development and Tourism Minister in a Congress government. Then in June 2011 he won the by-election to the Mukto Assembly seat that is still synonymous with his father's name. In July 2016, the State's political uncertainty made Mr. Khandu a surer leader when he took over from Nabam Tuki as the then Chief Minister of a Congress government. The assembly elections-2019 in Arunachal Pradesh were held for 57 seats. The BJP had won 38 of the 57 seats in the election held on April 11, 2019. Counting was held in 57 of the 60 seats as three BJP candidates had won unopposed before elections were held on April 11. In the second spot was new entrant Janata Dal(U) with seven seats.

AFSPA Withdrawn Partially from Arunachal Pradesh

On the Armed Forces (Special Powers) Act (AFSPA) was partially removed from three of nine districts of Arunachal Pradesh but would remain in force in the areas bordering Myanmar. The State of Arunachal Pradesh had inherited AFSPA since the day of its formation. AFSPA enacted by Parliament in 1958 and was applied to the entire State of Assam and the Union Territory of Manipur. After Arunachal Pradesh, Meghalaya, Mizoram and Nagaland came into being, the Act was appropriately adapted to apply to these states as well. Section 4 of the AFSPA empowers an authorised officer in a disturbed area with certain powers. The authorised officer has the power to open fire at any individual even if it results in death if the individual violates laws which prohibit (a) the assembly of five or more persons; or (b) carrying of weapons. However, the officer has to give a warning before opening fire. The authorised officer is also empowered to (a) arrest without a warrant; and (b) seize and search without any warrant any premise in order to make an arrest or recovery of hostages, arms and ammunition.

Arunachal has 35% of India's Graphite Deposits: GSI Report

The Geological Survey of India (GSI) in its report revealed that about 35% of India's total Graphite reserves is found in Arunachal Pradesh. This is the highest found in country. The GSI presented the said data during its annual interactive meeting with the Department of Geology and Mining & Industries, Government of Arunachal Pradesh in Itanagar (Arunachal Pradesh Capital) on May 16, 2019. At present India imports majority of Graphite from other countries. With 35% of India's Graphite deposits being found in Arunachal Pradesh, the State could now be developed as leading producer of graphite in country thus helping in meeting its future needs. The Arunachal Pradesh's secretary of Department of Geology and Mining suggested that the survey and drilling activities of GSI should be moved towards India-China international Border. As per the reports China is undertaking huge graphite mining activities across the border in Tibet Autonomous Region. Therefore, road and infrastructure development towards the (Sino-India) international border should act as a boon for exploration and extraction of mineral at the same time meeting India needs and reducing imports.

Pakke Paga Hornbill Festival Declared 'State Festival'

On 20th January 2019, Arunachal Pradesh Chief Minister, Pema Khandu declared Pakke Paga Hornbill Festival (PPHF) as the "State Festival" during a valedictory ceremony of the fourth edition of the festival at Seijosa in East Kameng district, Arunachal Pradesh. Pakke Paga Hornbill Festival (PPHF) is only conservation festival of Arunachal Pradesh. Pema Khandu announced that Arunachal Pradesh Forest Department will fund the festival from next year and permanent infrastructure will be constructed for the festival ground. In the PPHF festival is celebrated for the first time in 2015 to recognize the role played by the resident Nyishi tribe in conserving hornbills in the Pakke Tiger Reserve (PTR). The festival also provides an alternate source of income to the native people of the region who mainly relies on hunting and logging.

Arunachal Pradesh

GENERAL KNOWLEDGE

1 | Arunachal Pradesh: At a Glance

Area (in sq. km.)	: 83,743
Latitude	: 26°30°N to 29°30'°N
Longitude	: 91°30'°E to 97°30'°E
Forest Area	: 66,964 sq. km (79.96% of State's Geographic Area)
No. of Districts	: 25
No. of Sub-Divisions	: 45
No. of C.D. Blocks	: 99
No. of Circles	: 188

Names of the Districts :
- Tawang
- West Kameng
- East Kameng
- Papum Pare
- Lower Subansiri
- Upper Subansiri
- East Siang
- West Siang
- Upper Siang
- Dibang Valley
- Lower Dibang Valley
- Lohit
- Changlang
- Tirap
- Kurung Kumey
- Anjaw.
- Longding
- Namsai
- Kra Daadi
- Siang
- Lower Siang
- Kamle
- Pakke-Kessang
- Lepa Rada
- Shi-Yomi

Major Towns :
- Itanagar
- Naharlagun
- Tawang
- Bomdila
- Rupa
- Bhalukpong
- Seppa
- Ziro
- Daporijo
- Along
- Pasighat
- Yingkiong
- Roing
- Tezu
- Namsai
- Khonsa

No. of Villages (2011)	:	5,589
No. of Lok Sabha Constituencies	:	2
No. of Rajya Sabha Constituencies	:	1
No. of Vidhan Sabha Constituencies	:	60
Nature of Legislature	:	Unicameral
Capital	:	Itanagar
Languages Spoken	:	English, Monpa, Miji and Aka
Total Population—2011 census	:	13,83,727
Males	:	7,13,912
Females	:	6,69,815
Percentage of S.T.	:	68.81 (2011)
Decadal Growth (2001-2011)	:	26.0%
% of Urban Population (2011)	:	22.93%
Literacy Rate	:	65.4%

Male Literacy Rate   : 72.6%

Female Literacy Rate   : 57.7%

Density (per sq. km.)   : 17

Sex Ratio (per 1000 males)   : 938

No. of Universities   : 2   I. Rajiv Gandhi University
                                      II. North Eastern Regional Institute of
                                          Science and Technology (NERIST)
                                          (Deemed University)

No. of National Parks   : 2   I. Namdhapa National Park,
                                      II. Mouling National Park

State Animal   : Mithun

State Bird   : Hornbill

State Flower   : Rhynchostylis Retusa

Major Tribes   : Adi, Nyishi (including Bangru & Puroik),
                                  Apatani, Bugun, Galo, Hrusso, Koro,
                                  Meyor, Monpa, Tagin, Mishmi (including
                                  Idu, Taroan & Kamman), Sajolang, Sartang,
                                  Tai Khamti (including Khamyang),
                                  Tangshang (including Muklom, Lonchang,
                                  Tutsa, Tikhak, Hawoi, Longri, Mungrey,
                                  Mushaung, Lungphi, Joglai, Ngaimong,
                                  Ponthai, Khalak, Longhai, Halley, Chellim,
                                  Shechu, Shiangwal, Rera, Shiangtee, Dohe,
                                  Moital, Hatseng, Gajee, Gaja, Kochong,
                                  Lowchang, Laki, Gallon, Chamchang,
                                  Ringkhu, Shohra, Bowngtai, Rongrang etc.
                                  of Changlang district and Nocte, Wanchoo
                                  and Tutsa of Tirap district), Yobin, Singpho,
                                  Sherdukpen, Khamba, Memba.

National Highways passing   : NH-52, NH-52A, NH-153
through the state

Highest Peak in the State   : Kangte (7090 mts. MSL), in West Kameng
                                  District

Important Minerals   : Dolomite, Graphite, Coal, Quartzite,
                                  Limestone, Crude Oil, Natural Gas, Yellow
                                  Ochre, Marble.

Other Natural Potential	: Abundant forest resources and hydro-power potential.
Important Wild Life	: ***Animals:*** Mithun, Elephant, Tiger, Leopard, White Browed Gibbon, Red Panthers, Musk Deer.
	Birds: Hornbill, White Winged Duck, Green Pigeon, Sclater monal, Bengal Florican, Temminick's Tragopan.
Important Festivals	: Mopin, Solung, Nyokum, Lossar, Si-Donyi, Boori-boot, Dree, Reh, Sipong Yong, Chalo-loku, Kshyatsowai, Tamladu, Sarok, Nichido, Sangken, Mopin, Oriah etc.
National Parks	: Namdapha, Mouling
Main Rivers	: Siang, Kameng, Subansiri, Kamla, Siyum, Dibang, Lohit, Noa-Dihing, Kamlang, Tirap.
Places of Historical & Tourist Interest	: Bhismaknagar, Malinithan, Parashuram Kund, Itanagar, Tawang Monastery, Namdapha Wild life Sanctuary, Tippi, Orchid Centre, Akashiganga.

THREE NEW DISTRICTS

Arunachal Pradesh Legislative assembly on August 29, 2018 passed Arunachal Pradesh Re-Organisation of Districts (Amendment) Bill, 2018 for the creation of three new districts, Pakke-Kesang, Lepa Rada and Shi Yomi in the state.

1. **Pakke-Kessang:** It is carved out of East Kameng district with five administrative units namely Pakke-Kessangn, Seijosa, Pijiriang, Passa Valley and Dissingn Passo with district headquarters at Lemmi.

2. **Lepa Rada:** It is created by bifurcating Lower Siang district with headquarters at Basar. It has four administrative units namely Tirbin, Basar, Daring and Sago.

3. **Shi-Yomi:** It is created by bifurcating West Siang district with its headquarters at Tato. It has four administrative units namely Mechuka, Tato, Pidi and Manigong.

2 | Administration

ARUNACHAL PRADESH attained statehood on 20th February 1987. The state is divided into Twenty five districts, each administered by a district collector, who sees to the needs of the local people. Along the Tibetan border, the Indian army has considerable presence due to the concern about Chinese intentions. Special permits called Inner Line Permits (ILP) are required to enter Arunachal Pradesh through any of it checkgates on its border with Asom. Capital Itanagar is located at an altitude of 530 meters above MSL.

DISTRICTS

The districts of Arunachal Pradesh alongwith their headquarter are given below:

S. No.	District	Headquarters	S. No.	District	Headquarters
1.	Tawang	Tawang	14.	Papum-Pare	Yupia
2.	West Kameng	Bomdila	15.	Upper Siang	Yingkiong
3.	East Kameng	Seppa	16.	Anjaw	Hawai
4.	Lower Subansiri	Ziro	17.	Longding	Longding
5.	Upper Subansiri	Daporijo	18.	Namsai	Namsai
6.	West Siang	Along	19.	Kra Daadi	Jamin
7.	East Siang	Pasighat	20.	Siang	Pangin
8.	Lohit	Tezu	21.	Lower Siang	Likabali
9.	Lower Dibang Valley	Roing	22.	Kamle	Raga
10.	Upper Dibang Valley	Anini	23.	Pakke-Kessang	Lemmi
11.	Kurung Kumey	Laying Yangtse	24.	Lepa Rada	Basar
12.	Tirap	Khonsa	25.	Shi-Yomi	Tato
13.	Changlang	Changlang			

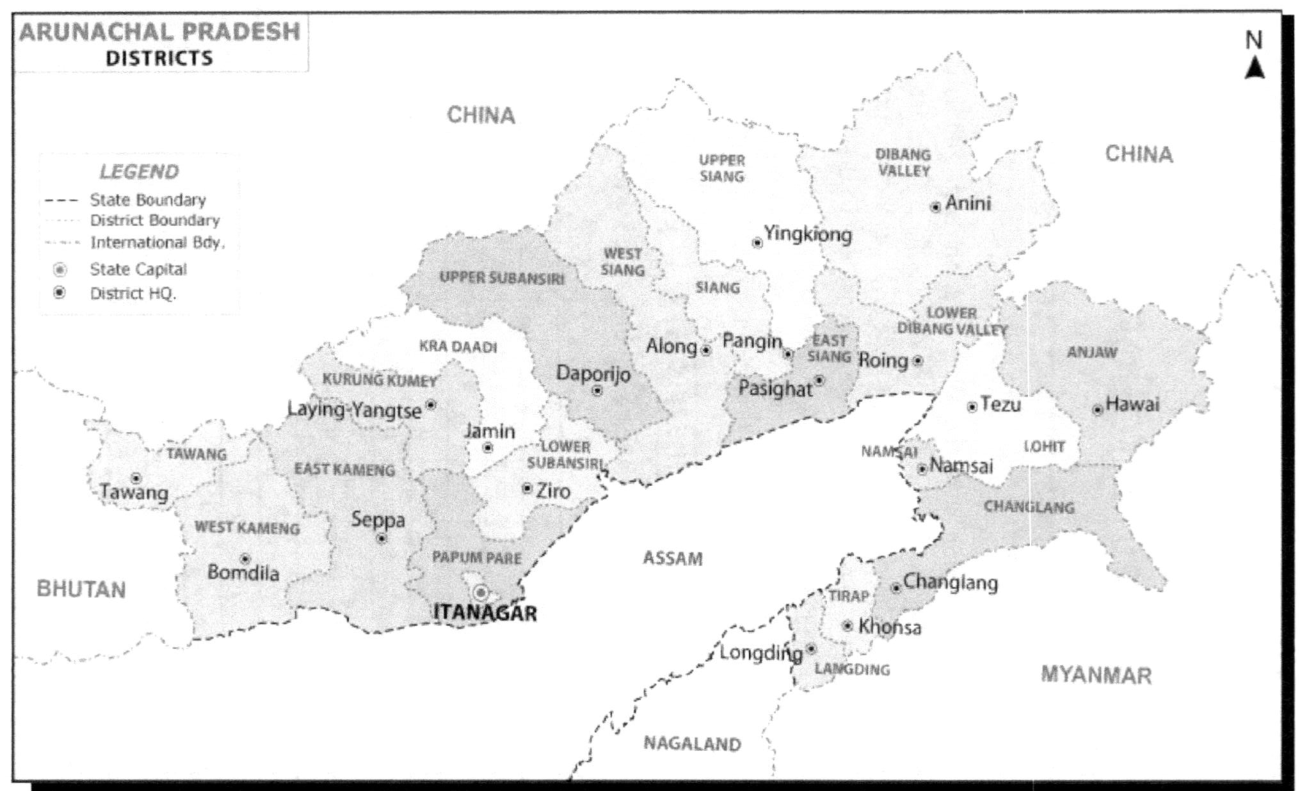
ARUNACHAL PRADESH
DISTRICTS
N
LEGEND
State Boundary
District Boundary
International Bdy.
State Capital
District HQ.
CHINA
CHINA
BHUTAN
MYANMAR
NAGALAND
ASSAM
UPPER SIANG
DIBANG VALLEY
Anini
Yingkiong
WEST SIANG
SIANG
UPPER SUBANSIRI
LOWER DIBANG VALLEY
Along
Pangin
EAST SIANG
Roing
ANJAW
KRA DAADI
Daporijo
Pasighat
Tezu
Hawai
KURUNG KUMEY
Laying-Yangtse
Jamin
LOWER SUBANSIRI
NAMSAI
Namsai
LOHIT
TAWANG
Ziro
CHANGLANG
Tawang
EAST KAMENG
WEST KAMENG
Seppa
PAPUM PARE
TIRAP
Changlang
Bomdila
ITANAGAR
Khonsa
Longding
LANGDING

It also possess 45 sub divisions, 99 C.D. blocks and 188 circles. Under the unicameral legislature system, it has 60 seats of legislative assembly. The state is represented in the Lok Sabha by two members and one member in the Rajya Sabha.

SOME INFORMATION ABOUT DISTRICTS

ANJAW: Anjaw was created on 16th February 2004 under The Arunachal Pradesh Re-organization of Districts Amendment Bill. The district borders China on the north. Hawai, at an altitude of 1296 m above sea level, is the district headquarter, located on the banks of the Lohit River, a tributary of the Brahmaputra River. The Mishmi, and the Zekhring (formerly called Meyor) are the main tribes in the district.

CHANGLANG: The Changlang district is located south of the Lohit district and north of the Tirap district. Changlang is populated by tribal groups, namely Tutsa, Tangsa, Nocte, Singpho and the Lisu. Sizeable communities of the Tibetans, Bodo Hajong and Chakma refugees do exist. The Namdapha Tiger reserve is located in this district.

EAST KAMENG: East Kameng district shares an international border with Tibet in the north, a state border with Asom and district borders with West Kameng, Papum Pare and Kurung Kumey, bifurcated from Lower Subansiri on April 1, 2000.

EAST SIANG: The district headquarters is located at Pasighat. Various tribal groups of the Adi people live in various parts of the district. The local people traditionally follow Donyi-Polo, although a sizeable minority has been converted to Christianity.

KURUNG KUMEY: Kurung Kumey is the newly-created fifteenth district of the state, with headquarters in Koloriang.

LOHIT: Lohit is an administrative district in the state. The district headquarters is located at Tezu. This area was one of the last territories to be brought under British control after the punitive Abor and Mishmi Expedition in the first decade of the 20th Century, and was known earlier as the Mishmi Hills. The district is named after the Lohit River, from the Sanskrit Louhitya, reddish- or rust-coloured, and consists of the river valley and hills / mountains to the North and South.

Lohit is the home of the Zekhring, Khampti, Deori, Singpho and Mishmi tribes. A small group of Tibetan refugees have settled in Lohit since the 1960s. The Zekhring are Tibetan Buddhists; the Khampti and Singpho are Theravada Buddhists, and the Mishmi are mainly Animists.

LOWER AND UPPER DIBANG VALLEY: The Dibang Valley district has been divided into lower and upper Dibang Valley for administrative convenience. The headquarters of the two districts are Roing and Anini respectively. Roing is a new-born town in the plains of the Mishmi hills. It is a beautiful place with picturesque nature and beautiful climate. However Anini is a hilly place lying in the mountains close to the frontiers of China.

LOWER SUBANSIRI: Lower Subansiri is an administrative district in the state of Arunachal Pradesh. The district headquarters is located at Ziro. The district has a population of 82,839 (as of 2011).

PAPUM-PARE: The district headquarters is located at Yupia. The district occupies an area of 2875 sq.km and has a population of 1,76,385 (as of 2011).

Papum-Pare is inhabited by members of the Nishi and the Mikir, who are traditionally followers of Donyi-Polo. Some members of the Nishi tribe are followers of the Baptist sect of Christianity.

TAWANG: Tawang Town is the district headquarters. The Tawang district is roughly located around latitude 27° 45' N. Elevations range between 6,000 to 22,000 feet, and inhabitants are found in lower altitude, where they enjoy a cool temperate climate.

The district was carved out of the West Kameng district, that adjoins it to the south and east. Bhutan borders Tawang to the west whereas Tibet Autonomous Region, China is to the north of the Line of Actual Control. The district occupies an area of 2172 square kilometres and has a population of 49,950 (as of 2011), almost 75% of which are considered "tribal", i.e. belonging to the native Monpa, Bhotia, Adi etc. In winter, Tawang frequently experiences heavy snowfall.

TIRAP: The Tirap district is located in the southeastern part of Arunachal Pradesh. It shares a state border with Nagaland and Asom, an international border with Myanmar and a district border with Changlang.

UPPER SUBANSIRI: Upper Subansiri is an administrative district in the state of Arunachal Pradesh in India. The district headquarters is located at Daporijo. The district occupies an area of 7032 sq.km and has a population of 83,205 (as of 2011). Members of the Tagin, Hill Miri and Adi are found in the district.

UPPER SIANG: The district headquarters is located at Yingkiong. The district occupies an area of 6188 sq.km and has a population of 35,289 (as of 2011). Various tribal groups of the Adi people and the Memba tribe live in the district. The Adi generally follow Donyi-Polo, and the Memba are followers of Tibetan Buddhism.

WEST KAMENG: It accounts for 8.86% of the total area of the State. The name is derived from the Kameng river, a tributary of the Brahmaputra, that flows through the district. West Kameng comprises five major tribes: Monpa (which makes up 78% of the district's population and includes Dirang, Bhut, Lish, and Kalaktang Monpa), Miji (Sajolang), Sherdukpen, Aka (Hrusso), and Khowa (Bugun). Minority tribes include Takpa, Lishipa, Chugpa, and Butpa.

WEST SIANG: The district headquarters are located at Along. The district occupies an area of 8325 sq.km and has a population of 1,12,272 (as of 2011). Various tribal groups of the Adi people, Memba and Khamba tribes live in the district. The Adi generally follow Donyi-Polo, although some have embraced Baptist Christianity in recent years.

Longding: Arunachal Pradesh got its 17th district Longding with the state assembly on September 26, 2011 passing out the 'The Arunachal Pradesh (Re-Organization of Districts) (Amendment) Bill,' 2011 by voice vote. Longding, the new district has been carved out of the Tirap district, and its headquarters Longding, one of the oldest sub-divisional headquarters.

Namsai: On August 15, 2014, Namsai was declared as the 18th district of Arunachal Pradesh. Just 75 km from Tinsukia Town, the major railway station, Namsai is fast developing as a township.

Kra Daadi: Kra Daadi was created as a district on 8th February 2015. It has been split from Kurung Kumey district. The district borders China to the north. Jamin is the headquarters of this district.

Siang: Siang District is the 20th newly created district of Arunachal Pradesh. It is predominated inhabitated by Adi tribe of Arunachal Pradesh. This new district was created by bifurcating West Siang and East Siang district. It came into existence on 27th November 2015.

Lower Siang: Lower Siang district, was carved out of West Siang and East Siang districts on 22 September 2017.

Kamle: A new distric called Kamle distric was created from Lower Subansiri Distric and Upper Subansiri District, with its headquarters to be located in Raga on 4 December 2017.

Pakke-Kessang: It is carved out of East Kameng district with five administrative units namely Pakke-Kessangn, Seijosa, Pijiriang, Passa Valley and Dissingn Passo with district headquarters at Lemmi.

Lepa Rada: It is created by bifurcating Lower Siang district with headquarters at Basar. It has four administrative units namely Tirbin, Basar, Daring and Sago.

Shi-Yomi: It is created by bifurcating West Siang district with its headquarters at Tato. It has four administrative units namely Mechuka, Tato, Pidi and Manigong.

ADMINISTRATION

The Government of Arunachal Pradesh works on the same lines as the other states of the country. The state follows a unicameral system of Government. It has only one house-the Arunachal Pradesh Legislative Assembly which consists of 60 members.

The political history of Arunachal Pradesh dates back to 1975 when it was made a union Territory (UT) with a separate legislative Assembly and for this purpose a Lt. Governor was appointed as the head of the UT. Later on in 1987 Arunachal Pradesh was made a full fledged state with 60 members in the state legislative assembly.

LEGISLATIVE ASSEMBLY

Origin And Growth

With the enactment of the NEFA Panchayat Raj Regulation (No.3 of 1967), the grounding for the Legislative Assembly of Arunachal Pradesh was prepared. This Regulation introduced a three-tier system: Gram Panchayat at the Village level, Anchal Samiti at the Block level and Zila Parishad at the District level. An apex Advisory Body, known as the Agency Council with the Governor of Asom as its Chairman, came into being on 29th December, 1969. A step further in the direction was taken with the enactment of NEFA (Administration) Supplementary Regulation, 1971 (No. 4 of 1971) which provided for replacement of the Agency Council by Pradesh Council and appointment of five Counselors', one from each District, who were in charge of various development departments. This Pradesh Council thus came into being on 2nd October, 1972.

As a natural outcome, the demand for a Legislative Assembly was pressed in every sitting of the Pradesh Council which made the Union Government to send a study team to assess the standard of Parliamentary acumen attained by the people of Arunachal Pradesh. The Union Government, after studying all aspects of the matter, agreed to the demand of the people for a Legislative Assembly, and on 15 August 1975, the Pradesh Council was converted into the Provisional Legislative Assembly of the Union Territory with all the members of the Pradesh Council becoming members of the Provisional Legislative Assembly and the Councilors being given the rank of Ministers.

Structure Of Legislature

Arunachal Pradesh has unicameral Legislature ever since its inception. The Legislative Assembly was consisted of 33 members, out of whom 30 were chosen by the people by direct election and three nominated by the Union Government. Consequent upon the formation of the State of Arunachal Pradesh with effect from 20 February, 1987 the total number of seats in the Legislative Assembly was raised to 60. The Legislative Assembly of the State, unless sooner dissolved, continues for 5 years from the date of appointment for its first meeting.

ARUNACHAL PRADESH POLICE

Having been constituted only in 1972, Arunachal Pradesh Police remains one of the youngest police services of the country. There are several historical factors for this delayed constitution of the force. In March 1976, the Government of India created a post of Inspector General of Police for this Union Territory. Shri K.P. Srivastava of U.P. Cadre assumed office as the first IGP of Arunachal Pradesh in March 1977.

In the year 1979, 4 more Police Stations started functioning. Since then there has been speedy process of modernization, development and expansion of the Arunachal Pradesh Police. On 20th February, 1987, Arunachal Pradesh acquired the status of a State and thereafter the force has taken rapid strides. The Arunachal Pradesh Police got the privilege of being headed by Director General of Police on Feb 13, 2002. Sh. Suresh Roy, IPS, 1968 batch of AGMU-Cadre was the first Director General of Police of Arunachal Pradesh Police. At present there are 3 Ranges, 25 Police districts, 71 Police Stations, 20 Out Posts and 25 Check Gates. The total strength of Arunachal Pradesh Police is 12024.

ARUNACHAL PRADESH PUBLIC SERVICE COMMISSION (APPSC)

Arunachal Pradesh Public Service Commission (APPSC) is a Constitutional body constituted with effect from 1st April 1988 under Article-315 of the Constitution of India. The Commission advice the Government of Arunachal Pradesh on all matters relating to state civil services and publish notifications inviting applications for selection to various posts as per the requisitions of the appointing authorities, conduct written tests and interview, prepare ranked list based on the performance of the candidates and advice candidates for appointing strictly based on their merit and observing the rules of reservation as and when vacancies are reported. The Commission is presently housed in the state govt. building located near Vidhan Vihar, Itanagar. The Commission consists of a Chairman, two members and a Secretary.

❖ ❖ ❖

3 | History

ARUNACHAL PRADESH means in Sanskrit "land of the dawn lit mountains". It is also known as "land of the rising sun" ("pradesh" means "state" or "region") in reference to its position as the easternmost state of India. Most of the people living in Arunachal Pradesh are either of Tibeto-Burman or indigenous tribal origin.

The history of Arunachal Pradesh has been traced largely from oral histories passed down from generation to generation, in verse and song. The Ahom buranjis (chronicles of the Ahom kings of Assam) and some archaeological finds that have been unearthed in the area have helped to reconstruct the history of Arunachal.

While the land has been inhabited since pre-historic times, it never came under the direct rule of the British nor indeed under the rule of any king in Delhi. The Ahoms did not rule over the hills of present-day Arunachal Pradesh, but, they did maintain contact with the people who lived there. Their primary motive was to protect their empire from depredation by the hill tribes, and to exercise control over the trade between the regions. Few trade routes passed through the hilly tracts to Tibet and, to China. Occasionally, they undertook a 'show of force' exercise, much as the British did, hundreds of years later. The Ahoms introduced a system of paying *posa* (literally money) to some tribes, to buy peace.

Archaeological finds in Dibang Valley (at Rukmaninagar and Bhishmaknagar), the copper temples at Tamreswari and Parashuramkund in Lohit district, the ruins of the Bhalukpung Fort, and the Ita Fort in Papum Pare, suggest some contact between the rulers in Assam (Asom) and the people of Arunachal Pradesh. By the 1830s, the British were firmly in control of the Brahmaputra Valley. Their approach to the hill people of present-day Arunachal Pradesh was remarkably similar to the policies followed by the Ahoms. By and large, the British Empire left the tribes alone, resorting to forays in the form of punitive expeditions only when their commercial and revenue interests were affected.

After independence, Arunachal was part of the North East Frontier Agency (NEFA) and later a Union Territory. On 20th February, 1987 Arunachal Pradesh was made a full fledged State.

BRIEF HISTORY

Except for the northwestern parts of the state, little is known about the history of Arunachal Pradesh, although the Adi tribe had legendary knowledge of the history. Recorded history was only available in the Ahom chronicles during the 16th century. The tribal Monpa and Sherdukpen do keep historical records of the existence of local chiefdoms in the northwest as well. Northwestern parts of this area came under the control of the Monpa kingdom of Monyul, which flourished between 500 B.C. and 600 A.D. This region then came under the loose control of Tibet and Bhutan, especially in the Northern areas. The remaining parts of the state, especially those bordering Myanmar, came under the control of the Ahom and the Assamese until the annexation of India by the British in 1858.

Heritage site, Bhishmaknagar, suggested that the Idu Mishmi had a local civilisation. Another heritage site, the 400-year-old Tawang monastery in the Tawang district, also provides historical evidence of the Buddhist tribal peoples. Historically, the area had a close relationship with Tibetan people and Tibetan culture, for example the sixth Dalai Lama Tsangyang Gyatso was born in Tawang.

In 1913-1914 representatives of China, Tibet and Britain negotiated a treaty in India: the Shimla Convention. British administrator, Sir Henry McMahon, drew up the 550 mile (890 km) McMahon Line as the border between British India and Tibet during the Shimla Conference, as Britain sought to advance its line of control and establish buffer zones around its colony in South Asia. The Tibetan and British representatives at the conference agreed to the line, which ceded Tawang and other Tibetan areas to the imperial British Empire. However the Chinese representative refused to accept the line.

Shimla Conference was initially rejected by the Government of India as incompatible with the 1907 Anglo-Russian Convention. However, this agreement (Anglo-Russian Convention) was renounced by Russia and Britain jointly in 1921, thus making the Shimla Conference official. However, with the collapse of Chinese power in Tibet the line had no serious challenges as Tibet had signed the convention, therefore it was forgotten to the extent that no new maps were published until 1935, when interest was revived by civil service officer Olaf Caroe. The Survey of India published a map showing the McMahon Line as the official boundary in 1937. In 1938, the British finally published the Shimla Convention as a bilateral accord two decades after the Shimla Conference; in 1938 the Survey of India published a detailed map showing Tawang as part of NEFA. In 1944 Britain established administrations in the area, from Dirang Dzong in the west to Walong in the east. Tibet, however, altered its position on the McMahon Line in late 1947 when the Tibetan government wrote a note presented to the newly independent Indian Ministry of External Affairs laying claims to Tibetan district (Tawang) south of the McMahon Line. The situation developed further as India became independent and the People's Republic of China was established in the late 1940s. With the PRC poised to take over Tibet, India unilaterally declared the McMahon Line to be the boundary in November 1950, and forced the last remnants of Tibetan administration out of the Tawang area in 1951. The PRC has never recognized the McMahon Line.

The NEFA (North East Frontier Agency) was created in 1951. The issue was quiet during the next decade or so of cordial Sino-Indian relations, but erupted again during the Sino-Indian War of 1962. The cause of the escalation into war is still disputed by both Chinese and Indian sources. During the war in 1962, the PRC captured most of the NEFA. However, China soon declared victory and voluntarily withdrew back to the McMahon Line and returned Indian prisoners of war in 1963.

INCEPTION OF ADMINISTRATION

Arunachal Pradesh acquired an identity of its own for the first time in 1914 when some tribal areas were separated from the then Darrang and Lakhimpur district of Assam to form North-East Frontier Tract (NEFT). The NEFT was further sub- divided into Balipara Frontier Tract, the Sadiya Frontier Tract and Tirap Frontier Tract between 1914-43. At the time of India's independence in 1947, the present territory of Arunachal Pradesh was under Part-B of the Sixth Schedule of the Constitution as the tribal areas of Assam. Part-B includes NEFT including Balipara Frontier Tract, the Tirap Frontier Tract, the Abor Hills district, the Mishmi Hills district and the Naga tribal areas. All these districts together were renamed as North-East Frontier Agency (NEFA) in 1951.

The NEFA was reconstituted under North-East Frontier Areas (Administration) Regulation of 1954 into Kameng Frontier Division, Subansiri Frontier Division, Siang Frontier Division, Lohit Frontier Division, Tirap frontier Division, and Tuensang Frontier Division. The Tuensang Frontier

Division was later separated from the NEFA in 1957 and merged with newly constituted Naga Hills which constituted a new State of Nagaland.

NEFA ADMINISTRATION

The NEFA was scheduled as part of Assam during 1950-65 and its administration was carried out by the Governor of Assam as an agent of the President of India under the Ministry of External Affairs, Government of India. Subsequently, the responsibility of the NEFA Administration was transferred to the Ministry of Home Affairs in 1965 as per the recommendations of the Daying Ering Commission (1965). Consequently, five divisions of the territory (Kameng, Subansiri, Siang, Lohit, and Tirap) became five districts. With the passage of time, these five districts have been further sub-divided into 25 districts.

POLITICAL PROCESS AND DEMOCRATIC DECENTRALISATION

Considering the recommendation of the Daying Ering Commission (1965), the North-East Frontier Agency Panchayat Raj Regulation Act was passed by the Parliament and put on implementation by the Government of India in 1967. As per provision in this Act, the Agency Council was formed at apex level followed by Zila Parishad at District level, Anchal Samiti at Block level and Gram Panchayat at Village level. The traditional village councils which were already recognized under the North-East Frontier Administration of Justice Regulation, 1945, were accorded the status of Gram Panchayats. The NEFA was upgraded as Union Territory of Arunachal Pradesh on 21st January, 1972 in pursuance of the North-East Frontier Areas (Reorganization) Act of 1971. Finally, the Union Territory was replaced by Pradesh Council which in turn was converted to Legislative Assembly in 1975. The first election to 30 members Assembly was held on 1978. Finally, the Union Territory was replaced by a full fledged State of Arunachal Pradesh (24th State of the Indian Union) on 20th February, 1987. The present strength of members of the State Legislative Assembly is 60.

INNER LINE REGULATION

The operation of the Inner Line Permit (ILP), which restricts the entry of outsiders into Arunachal, has meant limited interaction with the rest of India. There has, however, always been some interaction and trade between the hill tribes and the people inhabiting the plains of Assam. According to the provisions of the Inner Line Act, enacted by the British in 1873, people from other parts of the country cannot enter the State without the permission of the Government.

4 | Geography

ARUNACHAL (the Land of Dawn) is located in the extreme north-eastern corner of India. The word "Arunachal" means "land of the rising sun" or "land of the dawn-lit mountains" and "Pradesh" means "region". The State has a territory of 83,743 square kilometres, which is about 2.55 per cent of India's land area and a third of the area of North-East India (32.83 per cent excluding Sikkim). The largest State in North-East India, Arunachal's area is slightly more than that of Assam, but, its population is 0.11 per cent of India's population and only 2.85 per cent of the population of North-East India. All the States of North-East India, except Mizoram, have larger populations than that of Arunachal Pradesh. Itanagar is the capital of Arunachal Pradesh and located at an altitude of 530 metres above MSL. It is named after Itafort meaning fort of bricks built in 14th century A.D.

Much of Arunachal Pradesh is covered by the Himalayas. However, parts of Lohit, Changlang and Tirap, which are covered by the Patkai. Kangto (7090m), Nyegi Kangsang (7050m), the main Gorichen peak (6488m) and the Eastern Gorichen peak (6222m) are some of the highest peaks in this part of the Himalayas. In 2006 Bumla pass in Tawang was opened to traders for the first time in 44 years. Traders from both sides of the pass were permitted to enter each other's territories.

The Himalayan ranges that extend up to the eastern Arunachal separate it from China. The ranges extend toward Nagaland, and form a boundary between India and Myanmar in Changlang and Tirap district, acting as a natural barrier called Patkai Bum Hills. They are low mountains compared to the Greater Himalayas.

LOCATION

Arunachal Pradesh is located at the foothills of the Himalayan range in India. Statistically, Arunachal Pradesh's location is 26°30' North and 29°30' North latitude and 91°30' East and 97°30' East longitude. It is bordered by Bhutan on the west, China (Tibet) on the north and north-east, Myanmar on the east and south-east and the States of Asom and Nagaland to its south. Situated at the eastern end of the Himalayas, it is here that the Himalayan range changes its eastwest orientation to a north-south one.

Moreover, the location in Arunachal Pradesh has contributed largely to the tourism industry of the state. Drawn by the picturesque location of the state of Arunachal Pradesh, a large number of tourists come to Arunachal Pradesh to enjoy the celestial beauty of the nature in the foothills of the Himalayas. The hills, mountains and valleys adds to the beauty of the majestic state of Arunachal Pradesh and makes it location an envious one.

AREA

Arunachal Pradesh is situated in the North-Eastern part of India with 83,743 sq. kms area and has a long international border with Bhutan to the west (160 km), China to the north and north-east (1,080 km) and Myanmar to the east (440 km). The lofty slopes, turbulent streams, snow-clad peaks, sparkling rivers, etc.- all form an indelible part of the area in Arunachal Pradesh.

PHYSIOGRAPHY

Arunachal Pradesh is the eastern stretch of the Himalayas. The Himalayas constitute about 70,000 sq.km out of the total area of the state. The forested Shiwalik hills rise abruptly to 800 m above the Brahmaputra valley. Out of the total area, broad and narrow valley constitute 35 % each, the foot hills and the plain area cover 10% and the snow clad peaks cover about 20% roughly. The whole area may be classified into four belts from altitudinal point of view, viz., (i) foot hills below 3,000 ft. (ii) Middle belt ranging between 3,000-6,000 ft. (iii) High hills ranging between 6,000-11,000 ft. and (iv) Pastoral land and snow clad peaks beyond 11,000 ft. Arunachal Pradesh has two major sections, the Mishmi Hills and Patkai Bum (Range). The former contains the loftiest ranges with many summits rising above 5,000 m. There are several basins too. The largest, Taraoan basin is surrounded by several south flowing tributaries of Tellu river; in this basin the elevation of the hills ranges from 150 m to over 7,300 m. The hill ridges in Arunachal Pradesh are situated in a very haphazard manner. At these intervals, the wide and narrow valleys come into existence. Because of these ridges and valleys, the surface of Arunachal Pradesh is found varied almost everywhere which also results into numerous geographical isolations of pockets caused by various rivers and streams traversing the region.

CLIMATE

The weather and the climate of Arunachal Pradesh are quite distinct from the rest of the country. The climate of the State is dominated by the Himalayan system and the altitudinal variations. The climate here is highly hot and humid at the lower altitudes and in the valleys wrapped by marshy thick forest particularly in the eastern region, while it becomes too cold in the higher altitudes. Average temperature during the winter months range from 15 to 21 degree celsius and 22 to 30 degree celsius during monsoon. Between June and August the temperature sometimes go up to 40 to 42 degree celsius. The rainfall of Arunachal Pradesh in amongst the heaviest in the country. The annual average rainfall in Arunachal Pradesh is more than 350 cm.

RIVERS

Arunachal Pradesh is a land of lush green forests, deep river valleys and beautiful plateaus. The land is mostly mountainous with Himalayan ranges along the northern borders criss-crossed with mountain ranges running north-south. These divide the State into five river valleys : the Kameng, the Subansiri, the Siang, the Lohit and the Tirap. All these rivers are fed by snows from the Himalayas and countless rivers and rivulets except Tirap which is fed by Patkai Range.

The major rivers of the State are—the Brahmaputra and its tributaries (the Dibang, Lohit, Subansiri, Kameng, and Tirap). Much of the southern border follows the foothills bordering the northern fringes of the Brahmaputra valley known in Tibet as the Tsang-po, the great river curves around the Himalayas, to enter Arunachal as the Siang. The Brahmaputra flows eastward across Tibet before dipping south through the Himalayas into north-central Arunachal Pradesh. The river then winds its way southward across the length of the state, cutting a narrow, steep-sided gorge into the mountainous terrain. The Brahmaputra finally emerges on the Assam plains near the town of Pasighat. It is joined by the Dibang and the Lohit (another great river that originates in China) rivers (draining the eastern districts of Dibang Valley and Lohit, respectively) a few miles beyond Pasighat, just south of the Asom-Arunachal Pradesh border. West of the Brahmaputra, the Subansiri is the only tributary to cross the main Himalayan ranges. The Kameng (and other rivers in the area) rises on the southern flanks of the mountains. The Tirap River drains southeastern Arunachal Pradesh.

MINERALS

Geologically, Arunachal Pradesh is the least explored State and most of the mineral resources lie hidden underground. Major minerals found in Arunachal Pradesh are Coal, Dolomite, Marble, Lead, Zinc, Graphite, and Copper. On the basis of the explorations so far carried out by GSI, CIL, OIL, MECL, CMPDIL and APMDTCL, mineral reserves reported in Arunachal Pradesh are as detailed below:

Important Minerals

S.No.	Ores/Minerals	Location
1.	Coal	Namchik- Namphuk, Bhalukpong
2.	Dolomite	Rupa, Kaspi
3.	Limestone	Tidding, Pagin, Hunli, Menga
4.	Graphite	Bopi, Khetabari, Taliha
5.	Marble	Tezu, Dora, Hunli, Pyuli
6.	Lead & Zinc	Shergaon
7.	Oil & gas	Kharsang & Diyun (Kumchai)

ARUNACHAL PRADESH MINERAL DEVELOPMENT & TRADING CORPORATION LTD. (APMDTCL)

For conservation and explorations of vast minerals, the Arunachal Pradesh Mineral Development and Trading Corporation Limited (APMDTCL) was set up in 1991. APMDTCL is a wholly Govt. of Arunachal Pradesh owned Company. Main Objectives of APMDTCL are:

1. To search, prospect, explore, win, mine, quarry, dispose of and deal in minerals and mineral substances of every kind.

2. To arrange in the processing and manufacture of metals, metallic products, chemicals, cement and precious stones etc.

3. To seek, promote and operate schemes in collaboration with Arunachal Pradesh Government in a manner conducive to the balanced regional development of the various parts of the State.

4. To develop consultancy services in the field of mining, quarrying, procession, dressing, refining and others and act as consulting engineers and geologists.

MINERAL POTENTIAL VIS-A-VIS INDUSTRIALISATION

At present, Parsuram Cement Ltd. Tezu is the only mineral-based industry in the State. It is based on Tidding limestone deposits. Thus, APMDTCL is aware of the great need for taking suitable steps toward exploration and exploitation of the mineral resources of the State mainly with a view to set up more minerals based industries for its advancement. Proved reserves of mineral resources detailed above are capable of supporting following industries.

1. Fertilizer plant, refractory unit based on dolomite deposits.
2. Calcium carbide manufacturing unit and cement plant based on Tidding, Hunli and Pangin limestone.
3. Gasification and cooking plants based on coal deposits of Kharsang (Namchik-Namphuk) area.
4. Refractory, pencil, abrasives manufacturing units based on graphite deposits.
5. Cutting and Polishing units of decorative and building stones like granite, granodiorite, marble, and gemstones.

Production

The value of mineral production in Arunachal Pradesh at ₹ 252 crore in 2013-14 decreased by 21% as compared to that of the previous year. The value of the mineral production in the state was dominated by petroleum (crude) with a share of 80% and natural gas (ut.) 13% during 2013-14. The value of production of minor minerals was estimated at ₹ 16 crore for the year 2013-14. There was only a single mine reported of coal during both the years. The index of mineral production in Arunachal Pradesh (base 2004-05 = 100) was 152.1 in 2013-14 as compared to 165.8 in the previous year.

Mineral Production 2012-13 & 2013-14(P) (Excluding Atomic Minerals)

Mineral	Unit	2012-13			2013-14(P)		
		No. of mines	Qty.	Value	No. of mines	Qty.	Value
All Minerals		1		3186826	1		2521468
Coal	'000t	1	73	483600	1	—	—
Natural Gas (ut.)	m c m	—	41	339075	—	41	339075
Petroleum (crude)	'000t	—	121	2199269	—	111	2017511
Minor Minerals@		—	—	164882	—	—	164882

Note: The number of mines for petroleum (crude), natural gas (utilised) and minor minerals are not available. @ Figures for earlier years have been repeated as estimates because of non-receipt of data.

❖ ❖ ❖

5 | Agriculture

Agriculture is the mainstay of the people of Arunachal Pradesh and had mainly depended on Jhum cultivation. The principal crop of this area is rice, and other important crops include maize, millets, wheat, pulses, potato, sugarcane and oilseeds. The ecological conditions are suitable for horticulture and fruits like pineapple, orange, lemon, papaya, plum, pear, guava, cherries, walnut and peach thrive here.The Government of Arunachal Pradesh formulated the Agricultural Policy 2001 with the need for achieving higher economic growth and creating job opportunities for the rural unemployed through Agriculture and allied sectors.

The shifting cultivation which has come to be known as Jhuming which means collective farming occupies the central position in Arunachal Pradesh in the field of agriculture. This is the form of cultivation that sustains majority of the people in the area which has been practised from earlier days.

Arunachal Pradesh is one of the few backward states in the North-East which still uses primitive and obsolete technologies in agriculture. Use of plough and bullocks in certain areas of state is just a recent phenomenon. Cultivators continue to use dao (sickle) and dibbling sticks as their agricultural implements for most of their agricultural operations. Use of modern technologies like tractors, power tillers, etc., are limited to few very rich farmers. Due to unavailability of large flat tract this is not feasible too. Owing to the preponderance of forests, barren and uncultivated lands, Per Capita availability of land for cultivation in the hill areas of the state is lowest in India - only 0.12 ha. Cultivation has been extended to marginal lands through extensive deforestation resulting in low productivity and soil erosion.

Out of the net cropped area of 2.01 lakh ha, 60% falls under Jhuming (Shifting Cultivation) and rest under upland terraces, wetland terraces, valley lands and plains, etc. Rice accounts for a major share of 62.5% area followed by maize (16.2%) and millets (12.4%). In spite of high work participation (57.65% against 24% national average) of the rural people, average rice yield in the state is only 1.15t/ha, which is very low. Low solar energy interception, high rainfall, unfavourable water regime, undulating land, inadequate irrigation, uncontrolled water, low yielding and less responsive local varieties, low plant density and negligible use of improved tools and implements, fertilizers and plant protection chemicals—are some important causes of low yield and un-sustainability.

1. **Major crops:** Rice, Maize, Millet, Wheat, Pulses, Sugarcane.

2. **Major plantations:** Rubber, Coffee, Tea.

3. **Fruits, vegetables & spices:** Banana, Apple, Pineapple, Plum, Orange, Walnut, Guava, Grapes, Potato, Ginger, Chilli, Turmeric.

AGRO-CLIMATIC ZONES

There have not been much serious attempts at delineation of the entire region into specific agro-climatic zones. However, some attempts have been made based on altitude, rainfall patterns, temperature variations, topography, soil, etc. According to these criteria five agro-climatic zones have been identified in the state. These are:

(*i*) **Alpine Zone:** Gorichen, Upper Tawang, Tulungla, Bumla, Shela Pass area, Jidu and adjoining areas of northern Siang districts.

(*ii*) **Temperate and sub-alpine zone:** Tawang, Dirang, Bomdila, Shergaon area, Dibang valley, northern part of east Siang districts, Upper Subansiri district, part of west Siang around Anini and north eastern part of Lohit district.

(*iii*) **Sub-tropical hill zone:** Chngyak, Naga and Khonsa area and Basar area.

(*iv*) **Mid-tropical hill zone:** Southern part of Lower Subansiri district.

(*v*) **Mid-tropical plain zone:** Pasighat area and lower parts of Lohit district.

SOILS

The soils of Arunachal Pradesh have been formed from different type of parent materials. About 50 % of the area has been surveyed by the Geological Survey of India. The dominating parent material around Bomdila and Hapoli are found to be gneiss and granite rocks underlined with chlorite quart schist. The soils of the southern portion of Siang district have developed from basaltic rocks phyllitic to slaty rocks, massive quartzite and dolomite. Soil of Arunachal Pradesh is broadly classified into two categories viz., soils of the higher region and soils of the lower region.

The soils of higher region are developed from high grade metamorphics comprising of schist, gneiss, biotite granite, granodiorite, micaschist, hornblend, sandstone conglomerates, shales, phyllites, quartzites, etc. Soils are dark brown to dark yellowish brown in colour and are coarse to medium textured. They are coarse loamy sand to sandy loam with loam to clay loam sub-soil, where the depth ranges from 70 to 140 cm or more.

The soils are developed on the alluvium deposited by the rivers and colluvial was gliding down the slope and are carried away by runoff. These soils belong to the orders of Entisols, Inceptisols an Altisols tentatively. Almost entire soils in Arunachal Pradesh are low in available phosphorus and high in organic carbon content. The possible reason for higher organic matter content is due to thick forest vegetation, high rainfall and low decomposition rate. Soils of Kameng and Siang districts are medium in available potassium and that in Subansiri are rated low. The soils of the remaining districts of Arunachal Pradesh are high in Potassium. Practically entire soils of Arunachal Pradesh are deficient in available phosphorus. The reasons of low availability of phosphorus in these soils might be due to strongly acidic soil reaction and presence of considerable amount of exchangeable.

LAND USE PATTERNS AND LAND TENURE SYSTEMS

There is no land use/land cover map existing in Arunachal Pradesh. No exhaustive survey, either ground based or remote sensing is undertaken in this state to assess the pattern of land use or land cover. In many cases, inference is made about the land use pattern on the basis of crude estimation of land cover. According to the estimation of the State Forest Department, about 62% of the total geographical area (51,540 sq. km out of 83,743 sq. km) is covered with forests.

Most parts of land in Arunachal Pradesh are steep hills deep terrain and thick forests. About 62% of the land covered by forest is supposed to be the biggest endowment of nature. The rest of the land is put to different uses. About 34% of land which probably includes private lands reserved for hunting and fishing and residential areas, only 4% of land is presently available for agricultural purposes.

Land Utilisation Statistics

('000ha)

Lands & Area	2010-11	2011-12	2012-13
Fallow lands other than current fallows	70	69	69
Current Fallows	40	39	38
Net area Sown	213	215	216
Tota Cropped Area	278	281	285
Area sown more than once	65	67	69
Agri. Land/Cultivable Land/Culturable Land/Arable Land	424	424	424
Cultivated Land	253	254	254
Uncultivable Land	5237	5237	5237
Uncultivated Land	5408	5407	5406

Source: *Directo rate of Econimics and Statistics, Department of Agriculture and Cooperation Ministry of Agriculture and Farmers Welfare, Government of India*

JHUM CULTIVATION

Arunachal Pradesh agriculture is the main protagonist of the people out there and among all. Jhum cultivation means collective farming and it acquires central position in the agricultural sector of Arunachal Pradesh.

Jhum cultivation is the main occupation of the farmers in Arunachal Pradesh and it has been practised since past few decades. Majority of people in Arunachal Pradesh are dependent on this field of agriculture for their livelihood. Jhuming involves cleaning a particular portion of jungle by cutting off the trees and burning them and then sowing seeds in those clear areas with the help of a poker. Jhuming cultivation is practised in Arunachal

Pradesh agriculture after a certain lapse of years and the process is popularly known as Jhum cycle. Men, women, and children of Arunachal Pradesh everyone participates in this field of agriculture and put forth a hard labour that continues for around 5-6 months.

Jhuming is not only about cleaning the particular patch of forest but it revolves around a number of other agricultural activities as well. This agricultural activity of Arunachal Pradesh demands weeding for about 4 times at the least, observing the area and protecting the growing plants from wild animals and birds, and then finally cultivating a scanty amount of various crops. This farming of crops which demands such a huge amount of continuous labour do not really help the inhabitants much as the amount is very less to suffice the population. This makes Arunachal Pradesh a less active state in agriculture.

NEW AGRICULTURAL POLICY-2001

Arunachal Pradesh is slowly developing its economy with the objective of improving 'the quality of life of its people'. The task ahead are up hill, the resources available are plenty but the ways and means to achieve the objective through gainful utilization of the resources are not well defined. Technology has been relegated to the back resulting in stagnation of growth. However, the State has gained much over the years, it is now necessary to consolidate the gains in order to make it sustainable and add new dimension during the coming years, so as to increase household income generation.

Keeping all these factors in mind and the need for achieving higher economic growth and creating job opportunities for the rural unemployed through Agriculture and allied sector, it is necessary for the state to have a well defined policy. The policy should govern the entire gamut of Agriculture scenario of the State. Towards that goal, the new State Policy on Agriculture has to deal with the multifaceted problems and devise ways & means to redress them.

The major constraints are low level of productivity, capital inadequacy, lack of infrastructural support, unfavourable terrain, high cost of production along with demand side constraints.

The non availability of basic preservation, storage and processing facilities, low value addition and unfavourable price of Agricultural commodities are severely affecting agriculture as a whole which directly encourages migration from rural areas to urban centres.

The Policy Objectives

1. The new policy would accord top priority to increasing the incomes of farmers. This is necessary in view of the topographic disadvantages, communication bottleneck that hinders other income generating activities. The Policy, therefore, emphasizes all income generating activities like Cash crop, Floriculture, Fruit culture, Fish and Pig rearing, Agro-processing and so on along with all other activities that are considered necessary for the purpose.

2. Special emphasis to be given on shifting cultivation, ensuring better land management, introducing improved cultivation in slope land through Agro-forestry, Horticulture and encouraging other household activities. The programme is to be designed in such a way that there would be simultaneous thrust in weaning the Jhum farmers towards better cultivation.

3. Efforts would be made to formulate an area specific differentiated strategy taking into account the agronomic, climatic, socio-economic practices as well as the resource worthiness of the farmer. Special emphasis will be made for introducing the newly developed H.Y.V. seeds, improved planting material, adoption of new technology and mechanized farming.

4. There would be a shift from the commodity approach to system approach in Agriculture. All the land-based activities like that of Agriculture, Horticulture, Sericulture, Live Stocks, Fish rearing etc. would be given a new dimension and synergetic functional assignment. The ultimate objective is to create conditions which would help the farming community to maximize incomes. The policy will aim at avoiding duplication of programmes/ works by different functionaries, as far as possible. Towards that end, there will be regular monitoring and evaluation of all schemes implemented by Agriculture and allied Departments through appropriate mechanism.

5. Importance will be accorded to identify new location specific and economically viable improved species of Agriculture, Horticulture, livestock and Fish etc. Accordingly motivational aspect of Agricultural Extension would receive due attention. The entire extension system will be revitalized. Innovative and decentralized institutional change will be introduced to make extension system responsible and accountable. Development of human resources through capacity building and skill up-gradation of Extension functionaries will receive due attention.

6. Adequate and timely supply of inputs such as seeds, fertilizers, pesticides, Agri-tools and implements, credit at reasonable rate to farmers will be provided by the Govt. and other institutions, subject to availability of resources and funds. Greater emphasis will be given to increase the consumption of such inputs for achieving the targeted increase per unit area productivity. As far as possible use of organic manure/compost will be encouraged to avoid ill effects of inorganic fertilizers.

   Soil health card, quality testing of inputs like fertilizers, chemicals etc, will be introduced and supply of spurious inputs will be checked.

   On farm management of water, increasing the area under irrigation through use of surface water and sub-surface water will receive added attention.

7. Efforts would be made to create conditions that encourages participation of the private enterprises in the establishment of Agro-based industries. An incentive package and guideline would be finalised ensuring participation of private sector & financial institutions in the Agricultural sector as a whole. NABARD will have to play a major role in channelizing investment. To meet local credit needs of farmers, Rural Credit Banks are to be set up.

8. The new policy would encourage formation of "Self Help Group", village committees at different levels. The village committee would be vested with the task of maintaining and managing the assets created so far like irrigation channel, terraces, market shed etc.

9. Location specific Agricultural research, based on identified agro-climatic zone will be accorded foremost importance. Development of need based technology package for achieving higher productivity would constitute the thrust area of the new policy.

   Effort will be made to build a well organized efficient and result oriented agricultural research & education system for introducing technological changes in the Agricultural sector.

10. Emphasis will be laid on development of marketing infrastructure and techniques of preservation, storage, transportation etc. with a view to reduce the post harvest losses and ensuring a better return to the grower. Direct marketing and procurement by a notified State level procurement agency, as and when required with storage facilities of different items will be made available to the production areas. Upgradation and dissemination of market intelligence will receive particular attention. Efforts will be made to strengthen the market infrastructure.

11. Setting up of Agro-processing units in production areas will be given due priority. To reduce post harvest wastage, effort would be made to acid values specially to Agricultural and Horticultural produce by setting up small processing units. The Small Farmers Agricultural business Consortium (SFAC) will be activated to cater to the need of farmer entrepreneurs. Tea will be brought under Agriculture sector, but for processing it may be under Industries Sector.

12. Market intervention scheme involving procurement through a notified agency will be implemented for selected Agricultural/Horticultural Crops so that farmers are assured of remunerative prices.

Further, contingency agriculture planning would be encouraged along with the use of drought and flood resistant crop variety in the affected areas.

Agriculture in Arunachal Pradesh

S.No.	Item	Unit	As on	
			31.03.2008	31.03.2009
1.	Gross Cropped Area (estimated)	000 Hect	272	272
2.	Net area sown (estimated)	000 Hect	209	211
3.	Land under permanent cultivation	000 Hect	100	102
4.	Area Irrigated	000 Hect	54	55
5.	Area under Manure/fertilizer	000 Hect	26.5	29
6.	Area under HYV/Improved seed	000 Hect	70.0	72
7.	Area under Plant Protection	000 Hect	32	41

Source: Arunachal Pradesh at a glance 2009

Area and Production of Agricultural Crops in 2007-08 and 2008-09:
(Area in '000 Hect., Production in '000 MT)

Crops	As on March 31st		As on March 31st	
	2008	2009	2008	2009
Food grain	227	203	504.8	338.7
Pulses	8.5	8.4	8.6	9
Oil Seeds	30.8	31.8	28.5	31

Source: Arunachal Pradesh at a glance 2009

6 | Irrigation

I RRIGATION facilities have always been considered among the major inputs for permanent cultivation and better productivity. Except Apatani Plateau of Lower Subansiri District, Irrigation system was little known to the Arunachalees till 1950. Despite hilly terrain, low crop productivity and small land holdings, primary occupation of major population of Arunachal Pradesh is agriculture. Although the geographical area is larger than Asom, cultivable flat and mild slope area in the State is limited and hence every acre of irrigable land is to be planned properly to increase the productivity. Many farmers are resorting to shifting cultivation with primitive agricultural practices. In order to discourage the environmentally adverse shifting cultivation, permanent cultivation with assured irrigation facilities to the limited available area is the endeavour of the Government. The Government of Arunachal Pradesh, in line with the central government, gave its whole-hearted attention to provide irrigation for the cultivators. An area of more than 87,500 hectares has been irrigated in Arunachal Pradesh. 19% of total cultivated area is under irrigation.

MAJOR AND MEDIUM IRRIGATION

Topography of the State does not offer much scope for taking up Major Irrigation Projects. However, several feasible locations are available for Medium Irrigation Projects in the foothill and valleys of the State. The Detailed Project Reports/ Feasible Reports of following investigated projects have been brought out so far:

1. **Deopani Multipurpose Project:** Located in Lower Dibang Valley District, this project envisages irrigation potential creation of 5000 hectare CCA with power generation of 4 MW. Estimated cost of the project at 2004 price is Rs 77.03 crore. Its cost sharing on Irrigation and Power components are 57% and 43% respectively.

2. **Pappu Valley Medium Irrigation Project:** Located in East Kameng District, this project envisages irrigation potential creation of 2000 hectare CCA along with power generation of 750 KW. Estimated cost of the project at 2003 price is Rs 26.00 crore.

3. **Medium Irrigation Project at Paya, Hatiduba, Yealiang and Zeko Village under Sunpura Circle:** This project is located in Lohit District under Sunpura administrative circle. It envisages irrigation potential creation of 2170 hectare CCA and its estimated cost at 2001 price is Rs 13.30 crore.

In addition to above, one Medium Irrigation Project at Sille Remi in East Siang District is under survey & investigation in collaboration with the NERIWALM, Tezpur. This project is anticipated to cater irrigation potential of 2700 hectare CCA.

MINOR IRRIGATION

Reports of Minor Irrigation Census of the State reveals that about 1.20-lakh hectare (about 66.67% of available potential) irrigation potential has been created till the end of 4th year of Xth Five Year Plan. Geological fragility of Himalayan Region combined with highest rainfall intensity in the State result in frequent damages to the irrigation structures constructed earlier. Many minor irrigation projects have been rendered defunct due to water related damages. It is reported that about 30% of created potential (0.36 Lakh hectare) are lying defunct due to water related damages.

As against the potential creation of 1.20-lakh hectare, potential utilization is reported to be 0.48 lakh hectare, which is 40% of potential created. There exists a utilization gap of 60% at present. Expansion of area of utilization is done through the Command Area Development and Water management programme with active involvement of Water Users Associations in several commands.

COMMAND AREA DEVELOPMENT

Out of 1.20 lakh hectare net irrigation potential created, about 0.48 lakh hectare only has been brought under utilization. The utilized area works out to be 40% only leaving 60% potential created unutilized. With the help of Government of India, CSS Command Area Development Programmes are under implementation in a phased manner to narrow down the existing gap of 60%.

The irrigation potential created are brought under utilization through Command Area Development Programme. Under this programme, construction of on-farm-development (OFD) components like field channel, field drain, reclamation of water-logged areas within the command and correction of system deficiency are taken care of as hardware activities of the programme. It also covers regulatory water distribution activity called warabandi, formation of registered water user association (WUA), training to the officers and farmers as software activities of the programme. The programme aims at establishing a close partnership between the farmers (water users) and the implementing Govt. Department with the ultimate objective of transferring the responsibility of irrigation management system to the farmers.

FLOOD CONTROL

Flood menace in North-East is a recurring event. Monsoon brings sorrow and grief for Arunachal Pradesh. Due to high annual rainfall and geological fragility of the region, every year, the floods hit the State and render many people homeless, devastate agriculture, destroy road communication, towns and other public assets.

The first flood disaster in Arunachal Pradesh was observed in township of Sadia, situated on North bank of Brahmaputra (virtually the headquarters of erstwhile NEFA) in 1950 due to change in course of Digaru river. Due to high seismicity, high annual rainfall and geological fragility of the region, the process of erosion and flood related disasters recur every year. Population concentration of Arunachal Pradesh is mostly on river valleys, the towns like Seppa, Naharlagun, Daporijo, Basar, Along, Yingkiong, Pasighat, Roing, Tezu, Namsai, Miao etc. are on the banks of the rivers. The extent of damages caused by the flood is reported massive every year. Infrastructure development of the State has to go in tune with the existing characteristic behaviours of the river and therefore it is essential to develop a comprehensive master plan for structural and non-structural measures of flood management and its implementation is the foremost concern of the State.

BRIEF OUTLINE OF BASINS AND MORPHOLOGY OF RIVERS

Brahmaputra is a major international river covering drainage of 5,80,000 Sq.km, 50.50% of which is lying in China, 33.60% in India, 8.10% in Bangladesh and 7.80% in Bhutan. Its basin in India is shared mostly by Arunachal Pradesh (041.88%), Asom (36.33%), Nagaland (5.57%), Meghalaya (6.10%) Sikkim (3.75%) and West Bengal (6.47%). Within Arunachal Pradesh there are 10 major river basins consisting of 46 major and medium type rivers. The 10 major basins are:

1. Tawang River Basin
2. Kameng River Basin
3. Dikrong River Basin
4. Subansiri River Basin
5. Siang River Basin
6. Sisiri River Basin
7. Dibang River Basin
8. Lohit River Basin
9. Tirap-Dehing River Basin
10. Tissa River Basin

Numerous rivers originating from these basins ultimately drain to Brahmaputra River. This is a boon for the State for development of agriculture, power and industry sectors but at the same time these rivers have the destructive potentials unless certain preventive and protective measures are taken up in the State.

The Himalayan Rivers carry heavy sediment loads because of steep bed slope, soft and friable Himalayan rock. This is further aggravated by population growth with unscientific human activities on the valleys and high seismicity of the region. Consequent upon major seismic disturbance in 1950, large-scale landslide and heavy sediment transportation started. Rivers started braiding in the foothill area and this dynamic process is still actively continuing. Rivers of Arunachal Pradesh could be broadly classified into three types namely:

(*a*) Hilly reach (incised rivers)
(*b*) Foot hill submontance reach (boulder rivers) and
(*c*) Flood plain (alluvial rivers).

Flood related problems mostly occur in foothill submontance reach and flood plains. Population concentration of the State is also on these reaches. In the theoretical perspective, there are no flood inundation problems in hilly and foothill submontance reaches. Nevertheless, problem persists in these reaches not because of flood inundation but because of erosion that is equally as destructive as floods. Massive bank erosion takes place in every monsoon destroying crops, livestock, roads and bridges, other public assets and flood problem of Asom could be attributed to soil erosion within Arunachal Pradesh. The heavy silt-laden rivers coming down from steep slopes dissipate its energy at the flood plains (mostly foothill area of the State) and deposit silt on its beds due to which river water and excess silt spread overland causing braiding of rivers and submergence of agricultural land, towns and other public assets.

Flood Problems

Due to high seismicity and geological fragility of Himalayan geology and high annual rainfall, the state is highly vulnerable to water related disasters. The water related disasters in Arunachal Pradesh could be broadly classified into following categories:

1. **Soil erosion:** Because of steep slope in mountainous areas combined with human interference in the catchments area, large-scale soil erosion and bank erosion occur in agricultural field and dwelling areas. The massive soil erosion and bank erosion in the river basins of Arunachal Pradesh is the primary reason for the flood problems in Asom. In fact, this has inter-state ramification and Govt. of Asom with the Govt. of India should also focus its attention on the catchment treatment mostly within Arunachal Pradesh.

2. **Land slide:** Landslide is a common phenomenon in Arunachal Pradesh. Every year reports have been received from the districts regarding road blockages, mud slides in dwelling area, damages to irrigation structures and other public assets.

3. **Flood inundation and siltation:** Foothill areas of Arunachal Pradesh are mostly the flood plains of major rivers originating from mountainous regions. The hilly rivers flowing down with high energy dissipates its energy in the foothill region.

Irrigation Area (2010-11)

('000 ha)

S.No.	Item	2010	2011
1.	Net irrigated area	56	56
2.	Gross irrigated area	56	56
3.	Area irrigated more than once	—	—
4.	Net un-irrigated area	156	157
5.	Total Gross un-irrigated area	220	222

Source: Directo rate of Economics and Statistics, Department of Agriculture and Cooperation Ministry of Agriculture and Farmers Welfare, Government of India

❖❖❖

7 | Economy

A RUNACHAL PRADESH is the largest state in the North-East with a very low land-man ratio. It is known for its forest resources. The per capita income of Arunachal Pradesh has been the highest among the North Eastern states in the recent years and it has been above all India average. The main constraint faced by the state is the lack of communication. CMIE index for infrastructure development for Arunachal is 44, the reference point is 100, the National average. It is basically a hilly state that interspersed among deep valleys and narrow gorges. Forest products and industries based on them are the lifeline of the state providing income and employment to a large section of the Arunachalis. The state is rural based with nearly 75% of its total workforce is engaged in agriculture (mainly shifting cultivation). The remaining workforce being basically concentrated in the gradually emerging tertiary sectors. The secondary sector employment is mainly in the forest-based industries and also carpet making. Tertiary sector employment is mainly in the government jobs.

PER CAPITA INCOME

In a ranking of the States of India on the basis of their per capita income, Arunachal Pradesh is ranked in the mid-range. In the absence of data, the level of income in Arunachal Pradesh in the 1950s and 1960s is unascertainable but, since Arunachal was then a primitive agricultural economy, the income level was probably low. Formal estimation of the domestic product of Arunachal Pradesh began only in 1970-71. Thus, a comparative analysis of income of Arunachal Pradesh is possible for the last three decades for which the data on income and its structure is available.

In 1970-71, per capita income in Arunachal—more appropriately the Net State Domestic Product (NSDP) per head—was a little over half (56.14 per cent) the per capita national income. In subsequent years, the per capita income in Arunachal increased at a rate significantly higher than that of the per capita income of the country. The differential growth rate raised the ratio of per capita income in Arunachal to per capita national income. During the 1970s, the per capita income in Arunachal was 63.38 per cent of the per capita national income and, by the end of that decade, per capita income in Arunachal was around 75 per cent of the per capita national income.

Through the 1980s, Arunachal Pradesh moved faster than the country on the per capita income scale, and this closed the gap between Arunachal's income per head and the national average. By the beginning of the1990s, per capita income in Arunachal surpassed the national average. From 1991-92 to 1995-96, the per capita income in Arunachal Pradesh remained higher than that of the country. After 1995-96, however,the growth of income in Arunachal Pradesh has slowed down relative to that of the national income and, this is reflected in the falling ratio of Arunachal's per capita income to the average per capita income of the country. The last year of the 20th century, 1999-2000, ended with the per capita income of Arunachal at 84.64 per cent of the national average.

PRESENT STATUS

Territorially Arunachal Pradesh is the largest unit of the North-eastern region of India with 83,743 sq km of area. Geographically, it is situated in a disadvantageous position as it is not only a land-locked State, but is also surrounded on its three sides by foreign countries with total international boundary of 1628 km–1030 km in the North with China, 157 km in the West with Bhutan, and 441 km in the East with Myanmar. The states of Assam and Nagaland lie in its South. Like the other states of North-east, it is commercially integrated with the mainstream economy of the country.

In terms of Human Development Index (HDI) the position of Arunachal Praesh has been at the lower level. The State's HDI is only 0.501, a value which stands significantly below the national average of 0.577. Out of the 16 major states of the country whose HDI are available (HDR Report, Arunachal Pradesh, 2005), Arunachal Pradesh's position was 14th only above Bihar (0.449) and Uttar Pradesh (0.489).

To speed up the process of development in the State, the present 'inward looking' paradigms of developmental policy is to be supplemented by an 'outward looking' approach based on market and trade. The changing scenario in international trade under WTO regime, India's emphasis on signing trade agreements with several foreign countries including the South and South-east Asian countries (a few of which share common border with Arunachal Pradesh) and the 'Look East' policy of India can be of great help for Arunachal Pradesh in its efforts to introduce this 'outward looking' development strategy.

PROSPECTS OF TRADE WITH NEIGHBOURING COUNTRIES

The locational advantage of Arunachal Pradesh having common border with three foreign countries, viz., China, Bhutan and Myanmar can be of great help in following its trade-based and market-led 'outward looking' development strategy. China with its 9 to 10 per cent annual growth rate can alone provide good markets for several potential products of Arunachal Pradesh. In the past 25 years of expansion, China has lifted an estimated 300 million people out of poverty (less than 668 Yuan or about $60 a year). It is predicted by the Chinese Academy of Sciences that by 2050 nobody will remain below poverty line in China. The middle class will enjoy all affluent lifestyle. Arunachal Pradesh with a huge resource base can be one of the important providers of many of the items to be demanded by the emerging affluent middle class of China. Moreover, the rapid prosperity in the ASEAN region is also going to offer prospects for border trade of Arunachal Pradesh.

Arunachal Pradesh has potentials for producing some of the goods which currently India is exporting to various countries including those bordering Arunachal Pradesh. The name of some main items are Coffee, Fresh Fruits, Fresh Vegetables, Spices, Tea and Handmade Carpet.

China, the ASEAN region, Bangladesh and other SAARC countries which are geographically close to Arunachal Pradesh import substantial portion of each of the items in which Arunachal Pradesh has export potential. At present, Arunachal Pradesh is not in a position to exploit these potentials because of lack of awareness among the prospective entrepreneurs, crossborder transport bottlenecks due to closed border, absence of adequate investment for large scale production of these items for export purpose, etc.

PROCESS OF STRUCTURAL CHANGE

By structural change we generally mean how the share of different sectors of the economy to Gross State Domestic Product (at current prices) is changing.

If we see that the share of primary sector is declining over the periods and that of secondary and tertiary sectors are increasing, then a conclusion follows that the economy is moving in positive direction or the economy is moving in Kuznet's way. The contribution of agriculture has come down from 35 percent to 28.1 per cent, contribution of secondary sector has considerably improved from 19.1 per cent to 28.1 per cent. For tertiary sector, however the contribution has declined but it remained much higher in comparison to primary or secondary sectors. It is to be mentioned that though the contribution of primary sector has fallen but the people relying on it has not fallen neither in percentage or absolute terms.

The contribution of manufacturing sector is negligible and this proves the little existence of industrial activities. And most of the contribution to the State Gross Domestic Product. These two sectors primarily include different types of government jobs. Economy, outside agriculture is virtually run by Government alone and this may be considered as major deterrent towards achieving a self sustaining economy.

Sectoral Contribution to GSDP (At Current Prices)

(in percentage)

Sectors	1999 -2000	2000 -01	2001 -02	2002 -03	2003 -04	2004 -05	2005 -06
Agriculture	27.3	29.6	25.7	27.1	26.2	22.4	21.5
Forestry & Logging	4.3	4.8	3.3	3.1	2.2	1.9	2.0
Fishing	0.9	0.9	0.8	0.8	0.7	0.7	0.8
Agriculture & Allied	32.5	35.2	29.8	31.0	29.1	25.1	24.4
Mining & Quarrying	2.5	2.0	1.6	2.9	2.2	3.0	3.7
Total Primary	**35.0**	**37.2**	**31.4**	**33.9**	**31.3**	**28.1**	**28.1**
Manu-Registered	0.0	0.0	0.0	0.0	0.0	0.0	0.0
Manu Unregistered	2.9	3.1	2.4	2.6	2.2	2.2	2.4
Manufacturing	**2.9**	**3.1**	**2.4**	**2.6**	**2.2**	**2.2**	**2.4**
Construction	13.9	12.1	23.2	16.6	17.2	21.4	20.8
Electricity, Gas & Water Supply	2.2	2.1	1.8	2.6	6.9	8.7	8.7

Total Secondary	**19.1**	**17.2**	**27.5**	**21.9**	**26.3**	**32.3**	**31.9**
Transport, Storage & Communication	5.4	4.9	4.4	5.0	4.6	4.1	4.1
Trade, Hotels & Restaurants	5.9	6.4	5.4	5.8	5.3	4.8	5.1
Banking & Insurance	2.4	2.7	2.5	3.0	2.7	2.0	2.0
Real Estate Legal & Business Services, etc.	3.2	3.2	2.8	3.0	2.9	2.6	2.7
Public Administration	15.8	16.7	15.1	16.4	15.7	15.5	15.0
Other Services	13.3	11.8	10.8	11.0	11.2	10.5	11.1
Total Teritary	**46.0**	**45.6**	**41.1**	**44.2**	**42.4**	**39.5**	**40.0**
SDP	100.0	100.0	100.0	100.0	100.0	100.0	100.0

Pattern of Economic Growth

The economy of Arunachal Pradesh is roughly growing at an average of around 8 percent which is closer to the National average growth rate. By any measurement it is impressive but the question is which sectors of the economy are driving the growth. If the growth is primarily driven by the sectors where government is playing direct role then the sustenance of the economy will be in question. In primary sector the agriculture has achieved a compound annual rate of growth (CAGR) of 1.6 (from 2000-01 to 2005-06) and during that period population has grown at almost the same rate. It implicitly indicates low income base for the agricultural community and possibility of food scarcity can not be ruled out. Secondary sector has registered a healthy growth but it is primarily driven by construction. However, 2002 onwards, electricity, gas and water have registered phenomenal growth and contribution to GSDP has also increased in the same period, and it partially offsets the negligible contribution of manufacturing sector. In tertiary sector, the highest compound annual growth rate was achieved by public administration. The contribution of trade, hotels, banking and insurance, real estate and legal and business services to GSDP may not be on expected line but in terms of growth rate they are quite consistent. However growth is pronounced in those sectors where government is playing a direct role.

Sectorwise Real Economic Growth

(in percentage)

Origin of Industry	2000 -01	2001 -02	2002 -03	2003 -04	2004 -05	2005 -06	CAGR
Agriculture	13.0	-2.3	0.4	6.7	-3.5	2.0	2.6
Forestry & Logging	16.0	-25.0	-9.7	-22.6	3.3	4.1	-6.8
Fishing	3.3	5.2	0.0	2.0	9.0	3.8	3.8
Agriculture & Allied	13.1	-5.2	-0.7	3.7	-2.6	2.2	1.6
Mining & Quarrying	-26.3	-3.5	18.5	-7.8	15.3	25.7	2.0
Total Primary	**10.3**	**-5.2**	**0.3**	**3.0**	**-1.7**	**3.6**	**1.6**
Manu-Registered	0.0	0.0	0.0	0.0	0.0	0.0	0.0
Manu Unregistered	16.8	-6.2	9.9	-6.4	2.4	10.4	4.1
Manufacturing	**16.8**	**-6.2**	**9.9**	**-6.4**	**2.4**	**10.4**	**4.1**
Construction	-3.8	124.7	-30.1	14.3	38.9	1.0	15.9
Electricity, Gas & Water Supply	3.5	1.3	40.6	173.4	41.0	8.7	35.5
Total Secondary	**0.2**	**86.6**	**-21.9**	**30.2**	**36.1**	**3.6**	**17.9**
Transport, Storage & Communication	5.1	5.1	16.5	4.1	3.6	4.6	6.4
Trade, Hotels & Restaurants	19.5	0.2	4.2	1.6	1.2	11.0	6.1
Banking & Insurance	20.8	0.5	14.6	-4.6	9.9	0.0	6.5
Real Estate, Legal & Business Services, etc.	4.2	3.9	3.7	4.1	4.2	3.9	4.0
Public Administration	16.0	5.1	6.0	5.4	10.0	0.8	7.1
Other Services	1.9	8.0	-0.9	12.4	5.0	10.5	5.4
Total Tertiary	**9.5**	**4.8**	**5.5**	**5.8**	**6.4**	**5.2**	**6.2**
SDP	8.0	15.7	-3.9	10.6	12.2	4.3	7.6

FISCAL SCENARIO OF THE STATE

Before getting into the details of the fiscal scenario of the State, it should be mentioned that Arunachal Pradesh is one of the Special Category States which receive substantial financial and non financial support from the central government. It currently gets 90 per cent of its plan assistance as grants and the remaining 10 per cent as loans which is 30:70 for non Special category states. Special Category States receive preferential treatment in the distribution of normal central assistance from state plans. The Gadgil formula does not apply in the determination of the distribution between non Special Category States and Special Category States. Had the Gadgil formula applied on Special Category States, they would have been in disadvantageous position since the formula assigns higher weights to population and deviation of per capita income from the national average.

As it stands, fiscal situation in Arunachal Pradesh lacks buoyancy. It primarily depends on grants-in-aid from Centre. It is increasing by leaps and bounds, in 2001-02 it was 55.9 per cent of GSDP and it has reached to 89.7 per cent in 2006-07.The tax revenue collection in the state is very low. As a percentage of GSDP, it was mere 1.2 per cent in 2000-2001 and in 2006-07 it reached to only 2.7 percent. On the contrary, non tax revenue receipts have shown better result.

ECONOMIC GROWTH OF ARUNACHAL PRADESH

Arunachal Pradesh is the largest among the seven states located in the Northeast of India. Currently the state's economy is largely agrarian, based on the terraced farming of rice and the cultivation of crops such as maize, millet, wheat, pulses, sugarcane, ginger, oilseeds, cereals, potato, and pineapple. The state has considerable mineral reserves that offer huge potential. The state's hydropower generation potential is estimated at 60,000 Megawatt (MW), or approximately 25 per cent of India's current power generating capacity. As of June 2016, the installed hydropower generation capacity of the state was 97.57 MW.

The state's diverse topography offers ample of opportunities for non-timber based industries such as bamboo, cane and medicinal plants. Horticulture has a vast potential, owing to good agro-climatic conditions and topography, for the development of varied varieties of fruits and vegetables.

Between 2004-05 and 2015-16, the Gross State Domestic Product (GSDP) increased at a Compound Annual Growth Rate (CAGR) of 12.98 per cent to US$ 2.98 billion whereas the Net State Domestic Product (NSDP) increased at a CAGR of 12.59 per cent to US$ 2.62 billion.

The resources, policy incentives and climate in the state support investments in mining and mineral products (including cement), tissue culture and floriculture, plantation crops (tea, rubber, etc.) and agro-based industries.

The state's location provides opportunities for international trade with South Asian countries such as Myanmar, Bhutan and China. Textiles and handicrafts from the state are in demand in neighbouring countries.

The central government approved 'North East Industrial and Investment Promotion Policy' (NEIIPP), 2007 provides several incentives - incentive on business expansion, 100 per cent excise duty and income tax exemption, capital investment subsidy, interest subsidy and insurance premium reimbursement.

The Department of Industries has set up District Industries Centres (DICs) and Sub-District Industries Centres (Sub-DICs) for the industrial development of small scale, tiny and village industries.

Major initiatives taken by the government to promote Arunachal Pradesh as an investment destination are:

- The State Industrial Policy, 2008, of Arunachal Pradesh lists mineral-based industries (such as ferro-alloys, cement plants, etc.) as thrust sectors. Arunachal State Mineral Policy, 2014 has been prepared on the basis of the objectives of the National Mineral Policy, 2008. Arunachal Mineral Development Fund shall be created in accordance with this policy for its utilisation towards mineral exploration and development of mining activities in the state.

- The Government of Arunachal Pradesh plans to construct new roads and even connect the villages located at the India-China border. For the construction of this project, the Government approved an investment of US$ 555 million and the roads would cover a length of 2,098.40 km with 219 bridges.

- The Chief Minister's Skill Development Programme helped in improving employability of educated unemployed youth in the state. Its main objective is to provide 100,000 jobs for unemployed youths during the 12th Five Year Plan. Under this initiative, Job Mela-cum-Skill Development Interview Rally is being organised at regular intervals.

- The government has invited domestic power companies in the region to develop hydropower plants.

- The Ministry of Environment and Forests (MoEF) granted pre-construction scoping clearances to over 50 projects under the EIA notification 2006. Final environmental clearance has been awarded to 13 projects.

- The State Industrial Policy, 2008, provides incentives for developing tourism infrastructure, with a special focus on public-private partnerships in tour operations, hotels and resorts. The central government's Look East Policy is initiating tourism as a means to increase trade with other South East Asian countries.

- Under the 'Chief Minister's Paryatan Vikaas Yojana', a project has been launched to provide subsidised tourist cabs to educated unemployed youth across districts. For this, a provision of US$ 0.56 million was made during 2014-15. In 2015-16, foreign tourist arrivals in the state stood at 5,700.

FOREST ECONOMY

Forest has several uses and functions, which often compete with each other. Forests are scarce and are becoming increasingly scarce due to pressure on it. It can be attributed to increase in population and demand for forest resources. The forest resources of Arunachal Pradesh are under tremendous pressure due to increasing demand for human and livestock. Too much of extraction has led to forest degradation and disaster in ecological balance in recent time in this region and this led to famous Supreme Court verdict on 12/12/96 banning exploitation of forest resources specially industrial wood in Arunachal Pradesh and other States.

Forest revenue plays an important role in Forest economy of any state. The forest revenue of Arunachal Pradesh has decreased substantially specially after the Supreme Court verdict during 1996-97. The forest revenue during 1992-93 was Rs. 28.48 crores approximately while during 1993-94, it was Rs. 39.65 crores and Rs. 34.89 crores during 1994-95. It was Rs. 49.04 crores during 1995-96 and fell down to Rs. 25.24 crores during 1996-97 and further to Rs. 7.53 crores during 1997-98. There is some improvement in recent years while it was Rs. 15.61 crores during 2002-03 and Rs. 9.63 crores during 2003-04.

Forestry and logging sector played an important role in State Economy or Net State Domestic Product (NSDP) of Arunachal Pradesh. This is shown in table given on next page:

Contribution of forestry in State Economy of Arunachal Pradesh (at current prices)

Year	NSDP (Rs. crores)	Contribution of forestry (Rs. crores)	Contribution in percentage
1970-1971	21.34#	4.42	20.7
1980-1981	97.70@	9.99	10.2
1990-1991	231.11@	22.12	9.6
1991-1992	264.24@	22.39	8.5
1992-1993	271.07@	30.73	11.3
1993-1994	812.13*	93.24	11.5
1994-1995	872.68*	119.82	13.7
1995-1996	1071.45*	116.55	10.9
1996-1997	1082.71*	116.87	10.8
1997-1998	1192.18*	53.68	4.5
1998-1999	1353.82*	70.97	5.2
1999-2000	1457.08*	72.99	5.0
2000-2001	1594.86*	71.28	4.5
2001-2002	1730.21*	77.13	4.5
2002-2003	1744.36*	75.92	4.4
2003-2004	1970.66*	76.75	3.9

#At 1970-71 series, @ at 1980-81 series, *at 1993-94 series.

Beside the above, the forest based industries were closed down after the famous judgment and as a consequent 14 forest based industries out of 17 medium scale industries went to oblivion and as a consequence the contribution of manufacturing sector too had its impact in State Economy since 1997-98. The contribution of manufacturing was Rs. 36.17 crores during 1997-98 compared to Rs. 49.31 crores during 1996-97. It was Rs. 40.34 crores during 2003-04. Even the new industrial policy resolution of 2001 had very little impact in the manufacturing sector of the State.

❖❖❖

8 | Industry

The state has several medium industries based on its forest products. Plants to produce cement and fruit processing units have also come up in the state. There are a number of craft training centres and the state's handloom industry has made good progress. The people are experts in cane and bamboo basketry work. Wood carving and black smithy are found in certain villages. Iron scrapers, spear head, and Daos required for day-to-day use are made in several villages.

The Village and Small Scale Industries and Traditional un-organised industries constitutes an important segment of Arunachal's economy. This sector has not only continued to play to vital role in fulfillment of socio-economy objectives but also offer an excellent opportunities for the industrial self employment and is an ideal answer to the problem like un-employment and proper exploitation of available resources.

The aim and objective of the department of industries in the state is to promote the industrial activities in the state and thereby to provide employment opportunities to the rural and urban and to improve the economic conditions of the people. At present, there are 05 District Industries Centres and 08 Sub- district Industries Centres in the state.

The District Industries Centres (DICs) and Sub-district Industries Centres (Sub-DICs) play a prominent role for the industrial development of SSI, Tiny and Village Industries. This is an institution at the district level which extend all possible help and guidance to the prospective entrepreneurs for taking up of various industrial ventures in the district. Besides, these Centres offer all facilities to artisans, entrepreneurs and support them with maximum effort under single roof.

These Institutions are providing services like identification of suitable schemes, preparation of project report, arrangement for providing required plant and machineries and raw-material for entrepreneurs and marketing opportunities. Beside, assisting the entrepreneurs to avail themselves a series of package incentives and familities provided by both Central and State Govt. towards the rapid industrialization in the State. In addition to above, the DICs and Sub-DICs are not only acting as a co-ordinating agency but also maintaining close liaison with all Development Department and Financial Institutions in providing various assistance to the prospective entrepreneurs. As on 31-03-06, there are 13 Industrial Estates in Arunachal Pradesh. To provide training to craftsmen there are two industrial training institutes at Roing and Daporijo.

MAJOR INDUSTRIES

Arts And Crafts Industry

Arunachal Pradesh is a land of beautiful handicrafts comprising wide range in variety. All the people have a tradition of artistic craftsmanship. A wide variety of crafts such as weaving, painting, pottery, smithy work, basketry, woodcarving etc. are found among the people of Arunachal Pradesh.

On the basis of the art and cultural pattern, the indigenous inhabitants of the state may be divided into three distinct groups, (i) group comprising Bodic tribe like Monpa, Sherdukpen, Memba, Khamba, Khamti and Singpho, (ii) group including the Aka, Miri, Miji, Sulung, Nishing, Adi, Apatani, Hill Miri, Tagin, Mishmi, Tangsa, Nah, and (iii) the Nocte and the Wancho. All of these groups have some speciality in their art items. The members of first group are good in art of woodcarving and painting works. The second group is widely known for their weaving and cane and bamboo works. The third group viz. Nocte and Wancho are also good wood carvers but their style and motifs are quite different from the other groups. They also specialise in beads works. Apart from these, carpet making, tattooing, pottery, smithy and ivory works are also practised by some of the tribesmen, which assume significance of their respective society.

Weaving Industry

Weaving is the occupation of the womenfolk throughout the territory. They are very particular about colours and have a beautiful sense of colour combination. The favourite colours are black, yellow, dark blue, green, scarlet and madder. Originally they used natural dye but nowadays they switch over to synthetic dyes available in the market. The designs are basically geometrical type varying from a formal arrangement of lines and bands to elaborate patterns of diamonds and lozenges. These designs are enhanced by internal repetition and other decorations.

Few of the woven products that deserves mention are Sherdukpen shawls, Apatani jackets and scarves, Adi skirts, jackets and bags, Mishmi shawls, blouses and jackets and Wancho bags. Although fly shuttles are now being introduced particularly in the government run weaving centres, the traditional looms are still in use and the genuine textiles are products of these looms.

Cane And Bamboo Industry

Cane and bamboo industry of Arunachal Pradesh is of very high standard. Most of the domestic requirements are made of cane and bamboo. Hats of different sizes and shapes, various kinds of baskets, cane vessels, a wide variety of cane belts, woven and plains, elaborately woven brassier of cane and fibre, bamboo mugs with carvings, a variety of ornaments and neckless are some of the products that deserve special mention. The technique of basketry is also worth mentioning. The two basic techniques are twill and hexagon both open and closed.

Arunachal basketry is beautiful not only because of the fine texture but also because of the unusual shapes. Many a baskets have pleasing forms. There is definite correlation between the shape and the topography and climatic condition of the region. The angular and curvatious nature of some of the baskets has definite functional value.

Carpet Industry

Carpet making is the specialty of the Monpas. They weave lovely colourful carpets with dragon, geometric and floral designs. The choice of colour and the colour combination is unique. Though originally they weave carpet for domestic use, it has now become an item of trade. Along with increase in demand, production has also been made in large scale.

Wood Carving Industry

Woodcarving is a tradition with some of the tribes of Arunachal Pradesh. The Monpas, Khamtis, and Wanchos occupy significant place in this art. The Monpa wood carvers make beautiful cups, dishes, fruit bowls and carve magnificent masks for ceremonial dances and pantomimes. Wooden masks are also carved by the Khambas and Membas of West Siang. The Khamptis make beautiful religious images figures of dancers, toys and other objects. Very beautiful woodcarvings are made by the Wanchos of Tirap. In fact the Wancho area is the chief centre of woodcarving. Wancho woodcarving was earlier associated mainly with head hunting and human head dominated everything that they made. But nowadays variety of subjects is included. They are invariably free standing. Minute observation on the details will reveal that the Wancho wood carver has deep sense of proportion, in spite of the fact that they give much attention to the head. Of late departure from the traditional fixed form is noticed in many carved figures. Asymmetrical ones replace symmetrical postures; relief works are experimented in various themes. There is no doubt that change has penetrated deep into the Wancho woodcarving.

Ornaments Industry

Ornament making is another craft widely practised in Arunachal Pradesh. Besides beads of various colours and sizes blue-feathered wings of birds and green wings of beetles are also used in decoration. The Akas make bamboo bangles and ear ornaments, which are sometimes decorated with pocker work designs. Most of the ornaments are made of beads, as the tribes are very fond of it. While some people just hang strings of beads round their neck, others such as the Noctes and Wanchos weave them into very attractive patterns. The Wancho girls particularly are very expert in beadwork. The designs and colour combination are superb. Besides beadwork, the Wanchos make ear ornaments from glass beads, wild seeds, cane, bamboo and reed. Various ornaments of coloured glass beads hold a special fascination for the people of Arunachal Pradesh. Silver ornaments are a specialty of the Mishmis. The Idu Mishmi women wear silver fillet necklaces with lockets and beautiful earring. The Sherdukpens and the Khamtis at one time were also renowned for silver work.

Tourism Industry

The tourism industry has immense growth potential in the state of Arunachal Pradesh and the Department of Tourism, Arunachal Pradesh is making its best efforts to unleash the hidden potential and make the most out of it. Tourism industry in Arunachal Pradesh encompasses major sub types such as eco tourism, adventure tourism, wildlife tourism, historical tourism, cultural tourism and nature-based tourism. Arunachal Pradesh Tourism department is striving hard to promote the development of the tourism industry within the state and for that purpose has undertaken certain tourist-friendly developmental programs such as tourist guest house constructions at Ziro, Darak, Dirang and Zemithang, setting up of cafeterias at Dirang and Itanagar, construction of tourist view points at Darkang and Namdang and the like.

❖ ❖ ❖

9 | Horticulture

HORTICULTURE is the backbone of the rural economy in Arunachal Pradesh. It has a vast potential owing to varied agro-climatic conditions and topography for the development of varied varieties of:

1. Tropical, sub-tropical and temperate fruits
2. Spices
3. Aromatic and Medicinal plants
4. Mushrooms

Arunachal Pradesh is blessed with climatic and soil condition conducive for growing different varieties of fruits. Apples of Arunachal Pradesh are famous in the North-East and have made inroads in the Eastern Sector markets of India. Arunachal Pradesh is the largest producer of oranges in the North-East. Kiwis from Arunachal are now being sold in the Metros and production is increasing every year. Presently, the only problems being faced is in marketing it properly and lack of cold storage facilities. The government has made provisions for refrigerated vans so that fresh fruits can be made available in the markets year round.

Following table shows the status of Horticulture in Arunachal Pradesh.

Area and production of horticultural crops
(Area in ha.; Production in MT)

S.No.	Crop	2008-2009		2009-2010	
	Fruit Crops	Area	Production	Area	Production
1.	Apple	7320	10178	7686	10687
2.	Citrus	21829	27011	22920	28361
3.	Pineapple	8102	35841	8507	37633

S.No.	Crop	2009-2009		2009-2010	
	Fruit Crops	Area	Production	Area	Production
4.	Banana	4000	14717	4160	15452
5.	Walnut	2590	65	2719	68
6.	Other fruits	5733	17419	6019	18290
7.	Large cardamom	2480	578	2604	607
8.	Black pepper	738	166	775	174
9.	Other spices	7176	33185	7535	34844

Source: New Agricultural Policy, Dept. of Agriculture, Govt. of Arunachal Pradesh

❖❖❖

10 | Transportation

ROADS

Arunachal has a road density of just 25 km per 100 sq. km, as against the National average of 142 km. In comparison, Asom's road density is 87.22, Manipur's is 48.99 and Meghalaya's 37.8. In Arunachal Pradesh construction of roads really began in the 1960s, and starting from only 500 km, the road length increased to more than 15,000 km in 2000-2001.

Arunachal Pradesh is not fortunate enough to inherit infrastructure from the British Raj. At the time of independence there were less than 100 km. of dirt roads. At the time of attaining statehood in 1987, the total road length was only 3419 km. and today it stands at 18,000 km., a quantum jump in progress. The NH-52 and NH-52A have a total length of 380 km. in the State. The State is still quite deficient due to inadequate capacity, poor geomatric, poor riding quality, weak and distressed bridges and presence of a number of semi-permanent timber bridges and lack of wayside amenities. The present road density of Arunachal Pradesh is 25 km. per 100 sq. km. against all India average of 142 Km. per 100 Sq. Km. Out of 3863 villages, only 1743 villages are connected by road. Lateral road link is absent. There is urgent need to open up the potential and backward areas of the State through road connectivity for rapid economic development. Establishing continuity of connectivity by filling missing links, constructing bridges and protective/retention works is also one of the prime objectives of the State. Construction of Porter/Mule tracks/Foot Suspension Bridges along the rural link roads are also required to facilitate movement in the interior areas of the State as well as movement of defence personnel in the international border areas where taking up of construction of roads may take some more times.

The State's road network can broadly be divided into four categories, viz., (a) National High Way, (b) Major district roads, (c) BRTF roads and (d)

Rural roads.The major district roads run within the districts and across the inter-districts connecting districts HQs and other administrative centres. Rural roads mostly connect the villages. Notwithstanding the constraints and limited resources, the roads constructed by different agencies, viz., PWD, RWD, BRTF, BRO and Forest department working in the State upto 2006-07 are indicated below:

S.No.	Name of Agencies	Length (KM)	Type of Road	Source of funding
1.	PWD	6692.00	NH/MDR/ODR	State Plan/NEC/CRF/NH.
2.	RWD/Forest	4403.00	ODR/VR	State Plan/PMGSY
3.	BRO	4524.00	NH/MDR/ODR	NH/GS/CSG

Road Density And Surfaced Roads

The road density for the State is 25 km per 100 sq km. There is considerable inter-district variation in the percentage of surfaced roads as well as in the density of roads. Some districts have high road density, but, a low percentage of surfaced roads. Districts like Tawang, Lower Subansiri, and Upper Siang have a relatively low percentage of surfaced roads (all less than 40 per cent). Tawang has a high density of roads per sq km (48.75 km per 100 sq km), but, has a low percentage of surfaced roads (30.56 per cent), and Dibang Valley (Old) with a low density of roads (only 6.32 km per 100 sq km) but, has a high percentage of surfaced roads (62.83 per cent).

National Highways

Arunachal Pradesh has three national highways. They are:
1. **NH-52:** From Asom border-Pasighat-Dambuk-Roing-Paya-Tezu-Wakro-Namsai- upto Asom Border (352 km.)
2. **NH-52A:** From Asom border-Itanagar- upto Asom border
3. **NH-153:** From Asom border-Myanmar border (Still Well road) (40 km.)

Arunachal Pradesh State Transport Services (APSTS)

Arunachal Pradesh State Transport Services provides public transportation to passengers within the state and to the adjoining states of Arunachal Pradesh. Arunachal Pradesh State Transport Services-APSTS was started in the year 1975. It has approximately 200+ buses in its fleet providing transportation facility to the passengers in the state and to the adjoining states.

APSTS provides concessional services to the office-goers and Students. Free travel is allowed to blind/physically handicapped persons as well as to

Freedom fighters as per government policy. APSTS buses are available from following bus stations—Along, Bomdila, Seppa, Tezpur, Itanagar, North Lakhimpur, Ziro, Daporijo, Pasighat, Roing, Tezu, Namsai, Miao, Changlang, Khonsa. Buses are run on daily basis only on certain bus routes. Alternate day and nightly services are also run by APSTS.

RAIL: Arunachal Pradesh's capital Itanagar was put on the country's railway map on April 7, 2014 with the first passenger train carrying around 400 passengers arriving at Naharlagun. Itanagar is connected by Naharlagun-Dakargaon railway line covering a distance of 181 kms.

In a historic development, Prime Minister Narendra Modi on February 20, 2015 flagged off the first express train from Naharlagun in Arunachal Pradesh to New Delhi by pressing a button at a function held in Indira Gandhi Park in Itanagar. He had arrived in Arunachal Pradesh capital Itanagar to participate in the state's 29th foundation day. Modi, who was accompanied by the then Union Railway Minister Suresh Prabhu, Minister of State for Railways and Minister of State for Home, also inaugurated an intercity train between Naharlagun and Guwahati and laid the foundation stone of 132 KV power transmission project and another project to avail pure drinking water for the residents of capital town. Modi's visit assumes significance as the then President Pranab Mukherjee's visit to the state in 2014 had drawn sharp reactions from China, which has often laid claim to the state. "Arunachal Pradesh is the largest in northeast in terms of area. There is less population here but tremendous potential for growth. I assure you that you will witness more development in the state in next five years than it had seen in last 28 years," Modi said while addressing a huge crowd. The Naharlagun-New Delhi AC express train is a gift of the government of India to the people of Arunachal Pradesh on its 29th statehood day.

AIR: The state's airports are located at Itanagar, Daporijo, Ziro, Along, Tezu and Pasighat. However, owing to the rough terrain, these airports are mostly small and cannot handle many flights, they were actually used for transportation of food, when these parts were not connected by the roads.

The Arunachal Pradesh Helicopter Service operates regular services between Guwahati and Naharlagun. Helicopter services have also been introduced now connecting many other centres within Arunachal Pradesh. Services available are : Mohanbari-Naharlagun-Mohanbari; Mohanbari-Khonsa-Chanlang-Mohanbari; Mohanbari-Nafsai; Tezu-Nafsai-Tezu; Tezu-Roing-Tezu; Naharlagun—Ziro-Naharlagun, Ziro-Diporizjo-Ziro; Mohanbari-Pasighat-Mohanbari; Pasighat-Along-Pasighat; Along-Dambuk-Roing-Dambuk.

❖ ❖ ❖

11 | Electricity

POWER is an important element within the specific set of modern infrastructure components for overall development. In Arunachal Pradesh, the development of the power sector has assumed centre stage since the Sixth Five Year Plan when 12.82 per cent of the total Plan outlay was allocated to this sector. During the last two Five Year Plans, the efforts in this sector have intensified further. With its numerous rivers and streams, Arunachal has considerable potential for the development of hydroelectric power, but, this has so far remained untapped. So much so that a State, which has the potential to supply one third of the total hydroelectric potential of the country, is buying power at present, and close to 46 per cent of its power requirements are being met by diesel-generating sets. The Government is conscious of the situation, and is taking urgent steps to realise the potential that exists.

PERFORMANCE OF THE POWER SECTOR

The performance of the power sector in the State can be judged by examining four areas:

- per capita consumption of electricity,
- main sectors of consumption,
- rural electrification and
- cost of production of electricity.

The per capita consumption of electricity in Arunachal Pradesh was recorded as 144.78 KWH in 2004-05 against the all-India average of 411.04 KWH. This figure is lower than that in the other hill States of North-East India. The reasons for the low consumption rate are: low level of operational efficiency, low voltage operations, high operation costs, and irregular power supply in transmission lines. As far as the consumption of electricity in various sectors of the economy is concerned in 2004-2005, the largest share of electric power was for domestic purposes only.

In recent decades, electrification in rural areas has advanced rapidly; in 1971-72 only 37 villages were electrified. The number of electrified villages rose to 340 by 1980-81, and then to 1,308 (35.76 per cent) by 1990-91 and to 1,867 (60.46 per cent) by March 2005. However, the coverage of rural electrification varies widely among the districts, from 100 per cent in Tawang and Tirap, to 34 per cent in East Kameng. Block-level data shows that the blocks of Tawang, Tirap, West Kameng and Changlang have a relatively high percentage of electrified villages. The reasons for the relatively high level of rural electrification in these areas may be (i) both Tirap and Changlang are close to the Digboi and Sivasagar oil fields of Upper Asom that supply petroleum for electricity generation and (ii) Tawang and West Kameng have a cluster pattern of housing within the villages, which minimises the cost of electrification. On the other hand, some blocks like Bameng (East Kameng), Damin and Tali (Kurung Kumey), Giba and Nacho-Siyum (Upper Subansiri), Mechuka (West Siang) and Hunli-Kronli (Dibang Valley) do not have any rural electrification. Inaccessibility and scatteredness of the settlements are reasons for poor electrification in some areas.

The generation and distribution of power in the State is managed by the Department of Power, Government of Arunachal Pradesh. In 2001-02, the cost of production per KW was Rs. 3.12, and the cost of distribution per KW was Rs. 3.03. Against this, the average tariff charged from users was only Rs. 2.43. Thus, electricity consumption was subsidised by the State Government. At the same time, the transmission and distribution losses in the State increased from 30 per cent, in 1996-97, to a high of 51 per cent, in 2001-02. The reasons for such a high percentage of transmission and distribution losses are mismanagement, and inefficiencies in the distribution system.

The total installed capacity of the State has increased from 39.53 MW in 1994-95 to 57.66 MW in 2005-2006.The share of diesel-generating sets, as a source of power, has increased over the period, even though it declined in 2000-2001. In 2000-2001, 46 per cent of the requirement of power was met from diesel generating sets. (Diesel-generating sets are run by the Department to meet the power requirements of the State). The remaining 53.9 per cent of the power requirements was met by hydel projects.

Installed Capacity and Electricity Generated in Arunachal Pradesh

YEAR	Installed Capacity (M.W.)			Generated (M.W.)			Imported from outside the State [MU]
	Total	Hydel	Diesel	Total	Hydel	Diesel	
1997-98	53.88	23.83	30.05	89.29	69.25	20.04	78.84
1998-99	55.50	30.73	24.78	66.89	54.35	12.54	77.43
1999-00	65.57	30.57	35.00	62.21	52.10	10.11	98.89
2000-01	58.95	31.83	27.12	62.00	52.00	10.00	100.01
2001-02	59.60	32.48	27.12	60.00	49.00	11.00	94.37
2002-03	59.40	32.28	27.12	62.52	52.04	10.48	104.02
2003-04	59.60	32.48	27.12	66.50	56.18	10.32	302.56
2004-05	60.12	33.00	27.12	49.47	39.33	10.14	636.30
2005-06	57.66	32.66	25.00	52.07	43.94	8.13	317.47
2006-07	57.66	32.66	25.00	54.566	49.144	5.422	453.41
2007-08	58.71	33.71	25.00	55.31	50.67	4.64	571.071
2008-09	68.09	43.09	25.00	53.31	49.77	3.54	526.60

Source: Statistical abstract of Arunachal Pradesh, 2009.

Electrification in Arunachal Pradesh

ITEM	NUMBER
Total villages (2001 census)	3863
Village electrified (2005)	1867
No. of rural household (2001 census)	164501
Household having electricity (2004)	73250

Source: Rajya Sabha Unstarred Question No. 1863, dated 09.03.2006. Statistical abstract of Arunachal Pradesh, 2006.

POTENTIAL FOR HYDROPOWER

Arunachal Pradesh is extremely rich in hydel resource. Its hydro-potential is estimated to be more than 50,000 MW. Over 5400 MW of power would be surplus in the State by the end of 2022 if its hydro-power potential is totally tapped. The Department of Power has commissioned 35 mini hydel projects in different parts of the State. Out of an installed capacity of 463.95 MW only 57.66 MW (12.71 per cent) has been developed so far in the State sector. In the Central sector, 405 MW (87.29 per cent) has been developed by the North

East Electric Power Corporation (NEEPCO) by commissioning the Ranganadi Hydel Project.

More than a dozen projects are under consideration and are at various stages, ranging from the investigation stage to the construction and commissioning stage, with capacities ranging from 10 MW in the Dikrong Project to 11,000 MW in the Siang Upper Project. With the completion of the 405 MW Ranganadi Hydel Project, and the commissioning of other projects, the installed capacity in the State will be adequate to meet its power requirements, and Arunachal will be in a position to supply power to the rest of the States of North-East India and to neighbouring countries as well.However, the commensurate augmentation of transmission and distribution lines is crucial to ensure the optimal development of the power sector in the State. REL has entered into an agreement with the Government of Arunachal Pradesh for the development of two hydro projects—Tato - II (700 MW) and Siyom (1,000 MW) under a Build-Own-Operate-Transfer (BOOT) framework.

Some measures have been taken to reform the power sector in the State. A Regulatory Commission is in the process of being established. The State Government, the various Central utilities, and the Central Government have to act in tandem to reduce the inefficiencies, curtail the losses and thefts, and promote financial efficiency in the sector. Only then, will the power sector be able to attract private sector participation, and the immense potential in the sector can be realised. Given the precipitous topography, and the sparse spatial distribution of population, the conventional long-range generation transmission network may not suit Arunachal. Therefore, the provision of stand-alone isolated small generation facilities (50 KW to 4 MW) allowing for limited distribution in the habitation areas, would perhaps be more useful for capacity-addition, economy, and to contain the huge transmission and distribution losses.

Notwithstanding the State's immense potential for harnessing hydroelectric power, in view of its geological structure, and the vulnerability of the State's unique biodiversity (due to submergence by giant hydropower stations), the power development strategy for the State requires to be crafted very carefully.

Tailoring district-specific plans may be a feasible arrangement; for example, the improved design of waterwheels in Tawang, or the use of impulse turbines using high head in the rich catchment areas of Upper Siang, West Siang, and West Kameng, are options that need to be explored. In order to reap quick returns from the ongoing power projects, the State will need to invest intensively, within a span of two-three years, rather than spreading its resources too thinly.

❖ ❖ ❖

12 | Population

THE State has a territory of 83,743 square kilometre, which is about 2.55 per cent of India's land area and a third of the area of North-East India (32.83 per cent excluding Sikkim). The largest State in North-East India, Arunachal's area is slightly more than that of Asom, but, its population is 0.11 per cent of India's population and only 2.85 per cent of the population of North-East India. All the States of North-East India, except Mizoram, have larger populations than that of Arunachal Pradesh. The population density in Arunachal is 17 people per square kilometre (2011 Census). This stands in sharp contrast to the population density of 382 people per square kilometre in the country.

Population : At a Glance

HEAD	UNIT	2011 Census, Arunachal Pradesh
1. Population	Lakh	13.83
2. Decadal Growth	Per cent	26.0
3. Density	Per Sq. Km.	17
4. Sex-Ratio	Females per 1000 males	938
5. Literacy	Per cent	65.4
6. Urban Population 2011 (Census)	Per cent	22.93
7. S.C. Population 2011 (Census)	Per cent	0.6
8. S.T. Population 2011 (Census)	Per cent	68.8

According to the 2011 Census, the Scheduled Tribes (ST) population constitutes 68.8 per cent of the total population of 13,83,727 people, and the rest belongs to the General category. Some districts like Kurung Kumey have an extremely high concentration of the Scheduled Tribe population (97.89 per cent) while in Lohit district, the Scheduled Tribes account for only one-third of the population (32.42 per cent).

Districtwise Population, Decadal Growth Rate, Sex-Ratio and Population Density (2011)

State/Districts	Population 2011			Sex-Ratio (Number of Females per 1000 males)	Population density per sq.km.
	Persons	Male	Female		
Arunachal Pradesh	**1,383,727**	**713,912**	**669,815**	**938**	**17**
Tawang	49,977	29,151	20,826	714	23
West Kameng	83,947	46,155	37,792	819	11
East Kameng	78,690	38,775	39,915	1029	19
Papumpare	176,573	89,182	87,391	980	51
Upper Subansiri	83,448	41,758	41,690	998	12
West Siang	112,274	58,168	54,106	930	13
East Siang	99,214	50,116	49,098	980	28
Upper Siang	35,320	18,699	16,621	889	5
Changlang	148,226	76,948	71,278	926	32
Tirap	111,975	57,604	54,371	944	47
Lower Subansiri	83,030	41,843	41,187	984	24
Kurung Kumey	92,076	45,318	46,758	1032	15
Dibang Valley	8,004	4,414	3,590	813	1
Lower Dibang Valley	54,080	28,053	26,027	928	14
Lohit	145,726	76,221	69,505	912	28
Anjaw	21,167	11,507	9,660	839	3
Longding	—	—	—	—	—
Namsai	—	—	—	—	—
Kra Daadi	—	—	—	—	—
Siang	—	—	—	—	—

GROWTH OF POPULATION: 1961-2011

The indigenous population of Arunachal Pradesh started growing rapidly soon after Independence because of the falling morbidity and mortality in a very slow-falling fertility regime. Two factors—among many others—that caused the decline of morbidity and mortality can be singled out:

(*i*) the establishment of hospitals and a steady induction of modern health services; and

(*ii*) the smoothening of consumption, through the provision of food supplies, operationalised by the rationing system or the public distribution system.

The labour market in Arunachal Pradesh was absent among the local people, so, developmental activities, initiated by the Government of India, meant the in-migration of workers, both skilled and unskilled, from different parts of the country. This migration, which was only a trickle immediately after Independence, increased in the 1960s and 1970s, as the development process intensified.

Increasing in-migration added to the rising local population and led to an unprecedented growth of population, so that by 2011 the population of Arunachal was four-times what it was in 1947. Following table shows the growth rates of the tribal, non-tribal, and the total population of Arunachal Pradesh.

Population growth in Arunachal Pradesh

Year	Size of Population			Growth of Population (% per annum)		
	Total	ST	General	Total	ST	General
1961	3,36,558	2,99,944	36,614	–	–	–
1971	4,67,511	3,69,408	98,103	3.89	2.32	16.79
1981	6,31,839	4,41,167	1,90,672	3.51	1.94	9.44
1991	8,64,558	5,50,351	3,14,207	3.68	2.47	6.48
2001	10,97,968	7,05,158	3,92,810	2.7	2.81	2.5
2011	13,83,727	9,51,821	4,31,906	2.6	3.5	2.7

In the 1960s, the growth rate of the general population was very high,16.79 per cent per annum. In subsequent decades, while the growth rate of the general population declined, it was still high, indicating a positive inflow of population into the State.The tribal population grew faster in the 1960s than in the 1970s. There does not appear to be any plausible explanation for this, except perhaps an under enumeration of the tribal population in the 1961 Census. The other reason may be the inclusion of some Scheduled Tribes migrants in the Scheduled Tribes population of Arunachal Pradesh in the 1971 Census and their exclusion in 1981 (people belonging to the Scheduled Tribes elsewhere in the country are not counted as Scheduled Tribes in Arunachal Pradesh).

In the 1980s and 1990s, the growth rate of the Scheduled Tribe population increased and the growth of the Scheduled Tribe population surpassed the growth of the general population for the first time in the 1991-2001 decade. During the 1961-2001 period as a whole, the average annual exponential growth rate of the Scheduled Tribe population was 2.11 per cent while that of the general population was as high as 5.91 per cent.

The decadal growth of population in Arunachal Pradesh has been 26.0 per cent during the 2001-2011 period as against the all-India average of 17.7 per cent. This is a substantial improvement over the earlier decade, 1991-2001, when the decadal growth rate was 27.00 per cent against the all-India average of 21.34 per cent. The rate of growth of population in Arunachal Pradesh has been much higher than that of the country as a whole. During the four decades (1961-2011), Arunachal's population grew, on an average, at the rate of 2.98 per cent per annum against a 2.13 per cent growth rate for the country.

SEX RATIO

The sex ratio (defined as the number of females per 1,000 males) is a indicator of the health, nutrition, and survival status of women. The sex ratio in Arunachal increased from 859 women per 1,000 men in 1991, to 893 women per 1,000 men in 2001. More recently, it has increased to 938 in the 2011 Census. Among the districts, Tawang has the lowest and Kurung Kumey has the highest sex ratio.

The overall sex ratio in Arunachal is skewed due to in-migration. In order to isolate the effects of migration, we consider the sex ratio among the Scheduled Tribe (ST) population, which consists largely of the indigenous population. The ratio shows a steady decline in the 1961 to 1991 period,(from 1013 to 998) although it registered an increase in the last decade and has gone up to 1003 (per 1,000 males) in 2001.

Religion in Arunach Pradesh

Owing to its ethnic and cultural diversity, religion in Arunachal Pradesh has been a spot for thesyncretism of different traditional religions. Much of the native populations follow indigenous religions which have been systematised (generally following Hindu models) under the definition "Donyi-Polo" (Sun-Moon) since the spread of Christianity in the region by Western missionaries in the second half of the 20th century. The province is also home to a substantial Tibetanpopulation in the north and northwest who follow Tibetan Buddhism, of ethnic groups who subscribe to Hinduism, and other religious populations. Christianity is followed by over 30% of the population, mostly by natives.

Population by religious communities-2011 census

S.No	Religious Communities	Pupulation	Per cent
1	Christian	418,732	30.26%
2	Hindu	401,876	29.04%
3	Buddhist	162,815	11.76%
4	Muslim	27,045	1.9%
5	Sikh	1,865	0.1%
6	Jain	216	0.1%
7	Other (Mostly Donyi-Polo)	362,553	26.2%

13 | The People

THE people of this rich and colourful area are of many faiths and speaking many tongues. The Bangnis regard the Sun-Goddess as the chief divinity while the Sun and the moon are worshipped as the Donyi and Polo by the Adis and others. Major religions too are represented. There are the Buddhists of the Mahayana school in Lohit and Tirap; Buddhists of the unreformed Tibetan sect in Siang and the reformed one in Kameng.

There are some twenty major tribes each having a number of sub-tribes (numbering about 80 in all). The tribes inhabiting this region are—

(i) The Monpas, Mijis, Akas, Khowas, Sherdukpens and Bangnis in Tawang, West Kameng and East Kameng districts.

(ii) The Apatanis, Nishis, Sulungs, Hill Miris, Tagins in Upper and Lower Subansiri districts.

(iii) The Adis, which include a large number of tribal groups; Membas and Khambas in West and East Siang districts.

(iv) The Mishmis with three different sections, Khamptis and Singphos in Lohit and Dibang Valley districts.

(v) The Noctes, Wanchos and Tangsas in Tirap district.

☆ The Monpas inhabit the Tawang and West Kameng districts. They are a simple, gentle and courteous people and possess a high degree of culture. The Monpas profess Mahayana Buddhism and are distinguished for their terraced cultivation, carpetmaking and love of yaks and sheep. Their communal life is rich and happy.

☆ The Sherdukpens are of a small tribe living mainly in the two villages of Rupa and Shergaon in East Kameng. They are divided into two classes, the Thongs and the Gheos. The Sherdukpens are good agriculturists and traders. Their religion is an interesting blend of Buddhism and tribal religious beliefs.

☆ The Mijis call themselves Dhammai. In appearance and way of life there is little to distinguish them from the Akas (Hrussos).

☆ The Sulungs, one of the oldest tribes in the area, live in the high altitude of East Kameng district. They dress like the Nishis.

☆ The Hrussos are commonly called Aka, which means 'painted', for they have a custom of painting their faces with black marks. They figured frequently in old historical records. They are good traders.

☆ The Khowas (Bugun) occupy 7 villages in th neighbourhood of the Sherdukpens. The Khowas are also influenced by Buddhism.

☆ The Bangnis are divided into several exogamous clans. The Nishi men keep their hair long and tie it in a knot just above the forehead and they wear cane bands around the waist.

☆ The Hill Miris inhabiting the lower Kamla valley look attractive in their costume. They tie the hair in knots above the forehead.

☆ The Apatanis are settled in a plateau in the centre of the Lower Subansiri district, around the district headquarter. They live in crowded villages, are expert in wet cultivation and grow paddy in abundance. They have a stable agricultural economy.

☆ The Tagins, a hardy tribe, live along the banks of the Subansiri river (locally called Senyik) towards the north. They are hardworking and are expert in hunting. Agriculture is their main occupation.

☆ The tribes of the East and West Siang districts are mainly those classified under the general title of 'Adis'. They may be divided into three main groups : Gallongs, Padams and Minyongs, each of which can again be sub-divided into a number of sub-tribes.

☆ They are exogamous. Dances are very popular among the Adis. Ponung is their traditional dance which is also considered to be semi-religious in character.

☆ The Gallongs weave clothes of highly artistic designs and finest product is a beautiful skirt with a central pattern of black yarn netted in regular designs of black and white.

☆ The most striking features of the Padam and Minyong society are their highly organised political institution represented by the kebang or village council and the dormitory. They are forward looking, active and expert weavers.

✩ Along the international frontier in the Tuting area live the Khambas. They are Buddhists and lovers of dance. The Membas are found along the northern border of West Siang district. They are be religion Buddhists.

✩ There are three main groups of the Mishmis, viz. Idu, Miju or Kaman and Digaru or Taraon in Lohit district. With roughly 25,000 members, the Idu tribe is divided into sections, each named after the river by the side of which they live.

✩ It is in the manner of their hair style that the Idus are distinguished from other tribes. The hair in front is combed down to the brow and then cut straight across from ear to ear. The hair in the back is collected in a knot.

✩ The Mijus, unlike the Idus, keep their hair long. Their dress is a colourful as it is durable. Agriculture is one of the main occupations of these people. The Digarus call themselves Taraon. They are good agriculturists.

✩ The Khamptis live to the south of the Lohit district along the Kamlang, Dehing and Tengapani rivers with the Parasuram Kund to the north-east and Tirap district to the south. The Khamptis are good craftsmen, enterprising traders and skilful agriculturists. They are Buddhists.

✩ The Singphos live on the banks of Teang and Noa-Dihing rivers and extend towards the south-east into the land of the Khamptis. They are a fine athletic race with develped Mongolian features. They are expert blacksmiths and prepare iron implements of select brand. The ladies are good weavers. They are Buddhists.

✩ The Wanchos inhabit the south-western part of the Tirap district bordering Nagaland. They are fond of wearing decorated headgears and heavy strings of beads on neck, arms, legs and ears.

✩ The Noctes inhabit the central part of the Tirap district, to the north of the Wanchos. These people have long and traditional contact with the people of the neighbouring plains. Many of them are Vaishnavites.

✩ Tangsa is a common name for a group of people. These tribes occupy the eastern side of the central part of the Tirap district along the Indo-Burmese frontier.

District wise Population of Scheduled Tribes

Sl. No.	Name of District	Total Population	Total Tribal Population
	Arunachal Pradesh	**13,83,727**	**9,51,821**
1.	Tawang	49,977	34,811
2.	West Kameng	83,947	46,380
3.	East Kameng	78,690	72,400
4.	Papum Pare	1,76,573	1,17,216
5.	Upper Subansiri	83,448	78,323
6.	West Siang	1,12,274	92,783
7.	East Siang	99,214	69,979
8.	Upper Siang	35,320	28,468
9.	Changlang	1,48,226	53,878
10.	Tirap	1,11,975	98,372
11.	Lower Subansiri	83,030	72,911
12.	Kurung Kumey	92,076	90,764
13.	Dibang Valley	8,004	5,701
14.	Lower Dibang Valley	54,080	25,974
15.	Lohit	1,45,726	47,410
16.	Anjaw	21,167	16,451

Major Scheduled Tribes of Arunachal Pradesh

Abor; Adi; Adi Gallong; Adi Minyong; Adi Padam; Aka; Any Naga Tribes; Apatani; Bangni; Nyishi; Deori; Galong; Idu/Chulikata Mishmi; Khampti; Miji; Mishing/Miri; Mishmi; Monpa; Nishang; Nissi; Nocte; Tagin; Tangsa; Tawang Monpa; Wancho.

DISTRIBUTION OF TRIBAL POPULATION

As per the census 2011, there are 1,76,394 tribal households in the state. Total Population in the state is 9,51,821 of which males and females contribute around 49.2% and 50.8% respectively. The decadal growth rate of the tribal population during 2001-2011 is 35% which is higher than the state's decadal growth rate (25.9%). The tribal population of Arunchal Pradesh forms 68.8% of state's total population and 0.9% of country's total tribal population.

District wise Percentage share of State Tribal Population

Sl. No.	Name of District	Percentage share of state tribal population
1.	Tawang	3.66
2.	West Kameng	4.87
3.	East Kameng	7.61
4.	Papum Pare	12.31
5.	Upper Subansiri	8.23
6.	West Siang	9.75
7.	East Siang	7.35
8.	Upper Siang	2.99
9.	Changlang	5.66
10.	Tirap	10.34
11.	Lower Subansiri	7.66
12.	Kurung Kumey	9.54
13.	Dibang Valley	0.60
14.	Lower Dibang Valley	2.73
15.	Lohit	4.98
16.	Anjaw	1.73

SEX RATIO

Overalll Sex ratio among tribals are 1032 females for 1000 males. The child sex ratio is 977; it is lowest in Lohit and Debang Valley district (945) and highest in West Kameng district (1007). Literacy rate among tribals are 64.6%; among male it is 71.5% and for female 58%. Overall literacy rate is lowest in Tirap district (48.5%) and highest in Papum Pare district (79.8%).

LITERACY

Among STs, 64.58 per cent of the population has been returned as literate, which is just below the National average. Many STs have overall literacy level below 64.58 per cent. While male literacy is at 71.5 per cent, female literacy is only 58 per cent. The female literacy is depressed as seventeen STs have recorded literacy below 50 per cent. Papum Pare district have highest (79.77%) and Tirap district have lowest (48.51%) literacy rate. In Males Papum Pare have highest (85.98%) and Kurung Kumey have lowest (54.89%) literacy rate.

Districtwise Literacy rate of Scheduled Tribes

Sl. No.	Name of District	Literacy rate (7+ population)	Male literacy rate	Female literacy rate
	Arunachal Pradesh	**64.58**	**71.48**	**57.96**
1.	Tawang	51.79	59.59	44.63
2.	West Kameng	61.48	66.84	56.33
3.	East Kameng	58.66	67.28	50.57
4.	Papum Pare	79.77	85.98	74.08
5.	Upper Subansiri	63.19	69.21	57.43
6.	West Siang	64.55	70.25	59.09
7.	East Siang	76.55	82.41	70.86
8.	Upper Siang	58.02	63.75	52.16
9.	Changlang	68.90	76.52	61.21
10.	Tirap	48.51	58.19	38.82
11.	Lower Subansiri	73.97	80.50	67.72
12.	Kurung Kumey	48.59	54.89	42.63
13.	Dibang Valley	66.56	73.23	9.95
14.	Lower Dibang Valley	76.11	83.39	69.26
15.	Lohit	75.74	83.88	67.89
16.	Anjaw	51.60	62.10	41.17

RELIGION

Of the total ST population, 47.2 per cent has been returned under the category of "Other Religion Followers". Besides, 26.5 per cent of the STs are Christians, 13.1 per cent Hindus, and 11.7 per cent Budhists. In Arunachal Pradesh, unlike Nagaland, Mizoram, and Manipur, considerable ST population are still adhering to original tribal faith. Individual ST wise, Khampti, Monpa, Momba, Sherdukpen, and Singpho are mostly the followers of Buddhism, while quite sizeable population among Adi, Nishi, Nocte, and Wancho have been converted to Christianity.

Districtwise Rural and Urban Scheduled Tribes Population

Name of District	Area	Persons	Males	Females
Arunachal Pradesh	Rural	7,89,846	3,90,625	3,99,221
	Urban	1,61,975	77,765	84,210
Tawang	Rural	31,105	15,024	16,081
	Urban	3,706	1,746	1,960
West Kameng	Rural	38,846	19,104	19,742
	Urban	7,534	3,667	3,867
East Kameng	Rural	57,797	28,146	29,651
	Urban	14,603	7,120	7,483
Papum Pare	Rural	61,451	29,711	31,740
	Urban	55,765	26,758	29,007
Upper Subansiri	Rural	67,960	33,550	34,410
	Urban	10,363	5,020	5,343
West Siang	Rural	78,260	38,874	39,386
	Urban	14,523	6,872	7,651
East Siang	Rural	57,744	28,785	28,959
	Urban	12,235	5,748	6,487
Upper Siang	Rural	24,498	12,492	12,006
	Urban	3,970	1,921	2,049
Changlang	Rural	48,221	24,246	23,975
	Urban	5,657	2,815	2,842
Tirap	Rural	87,509	44,101	43,408
	Urban	10,863	5,264	5,599
Lower Subansiri	Rural	64,374	31,912	32,462
	Urban	8,537	3,891	4,646
Kurung Kumey	Rural	88,658	43,406	45,252
	Urban	2,106	1,053	1,053
Dibang Valley	Rural	4,480	2,285	2,195
	Urban	1,221	565	656
Lower Dibang Valley	Rural	22,579	11,024	11,555
	Urban	3,395	1,625	1,770
Lohit	Rural	40,355	19,964	20,391
	Urban	7,055	3,493	3,562
Anjaw	Rural	16,009	8,001	8,008
	Urban	442	207	235

Districtwise Sex Ratio of Scheduled Tribes Population

Sl. No.	Name of District	Total	Rural	Urban
	Arunachal Pradesh	**1,032**	**1,022**	**1,083**
1.	Tawang	1,076	1,070	1,123
2.	West Kameng	1,037	1,033	1,055
3.	East Kameng	1,053	1,053	1,051
4.	Papum Pare	1,076	1,068	1,084
5.	Upper Subansiri	1,031	1,026	1,064
6.	West Siang	1,028	1,013	1,113
7.	East Siang	1,026	1,006	1,129
8.	Upper Siang	975	961	1,067
9.	Changlang	991	989	1,010
10.	Tirap	993	984	1,064
11.	Lower Subansiri	1,036	1,017	1,194
12.	Kurung Kumey	1,042	1,043	1,000
13.	Dibang Valley	1,000	961	1,161
14.	Lower Dibang Valley	1,053	1,048	1,089
15.	Lohit	1,021	1,021	1,020
16.	Anjaw	1,004	1,001	1,135

14 | Flora and Fauna

THE recorded forest area is 51,407 sq. km constituting 61.39% of the total geographical area of the State. Out of this Reserved Forests constitute 20.60%, Protected Forests 19.02% and Unclassed Forests 60.38%. The four major forest types occurring in the State are Tropical Wet Evergreen Forest, Sub-Tropical Pine Forest, Montane Wet Temperate Forest and Sub-Alpine/ Alpine Forest.

PROTECTED AREAS

A total of 0.99 million hect. of the forest area constituting 11.82% of the geographical area is under two National Parks (2,290.82 sq. km) and 11 Wildlife Sanctuaries (7,606.37 sq. km). Arunachal Pradesh has two Tiger Reserves (Namdapha and Mouling) covering 2,847 sq. km. The Dehang-Dibang valley, with an area of 5,11150 sq. km, has been declared as a Biosphere reserve.

FOREST COVER

The forest cover of the state, based on satellite data of October-December 2015, is 66,964 sq. km, which constitutes 79.96% of geographic area. Very dense forest is 20,721 sq. km, moderately dense forest, 30,955 sq. km, and open forest, 15,288 sq. km. About one-fourth of the very dense forest of the country exist in the State.

A loss of 190 sq km has been recorded in the present assessment as compared to previous assessment. The decrease in forest cover is mainly due to shifting cultivation areas in the districts of Lohit, Changlang, Kameng East, Papum-Pare, Siang Upper, Siang West, Subansiri Upper, and Tirap as observed by the FSI officials during ground verification and development activities.

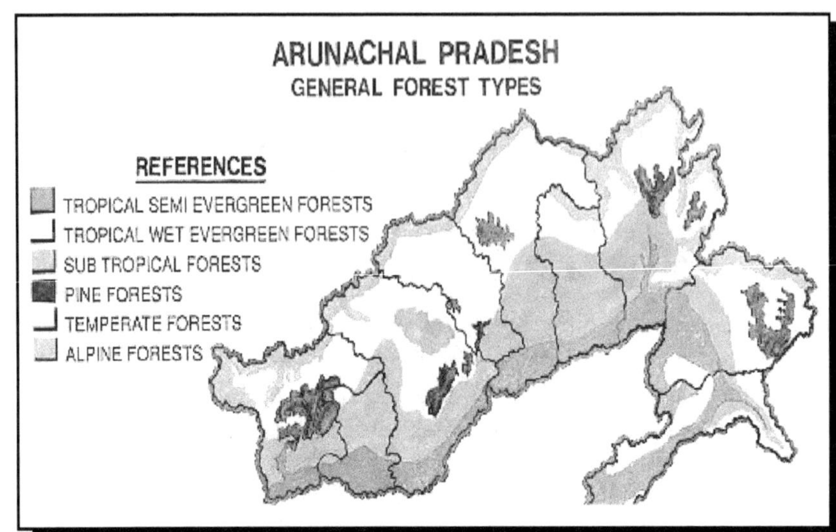

Forest Cover within and outside Green Wash

Forest Cover within Green Wash (Area in sq. km)	
Very Dense Forest (VDF)	19,095
Moderately Dense Forest (MDF)	27,629
Open Forest (OF)	11,876
Total	58,600
Forest Cover Outside Green Wash	
Very Dense Forest	1,626
Moderately dense Forest	3,326
Open Forest	3,412
Total	8,364
Total Forest Cover	**66,964**
Tree Cover	**807**
Total Forest & Tree Cover	**67,771**
Of State's Geographical Area	80.93%
Of India's Forest & Tree Cover	8.45%
Per Capita Forest & Tree Cover	4.91 ha

District-wise forest cover (in sq. km.)
2017 ASSESSMENT

District	Geogra- phic area	Very dense	Mod. dense	Open forest	Total	Percent of G.A.	Change	Scrub
Changlang	4,662	1,754	1,372	866	3,992	85.63	-30	5
Dibang Valley & Lower Dibang Valley	13,029	1,691	4,925	2,616	9,232	70.86	-35	8
East Kameng & West Kameng	11,556	3,433	4,667	2,178	10,278	88.94	-96	29
East Siang	3,603	881	1,268	731	2,880	79.93	6	10
Kurung-Kumey & Lower Subansiri	9,548	2,943	4,060	1,379	8,382	87.79	-20	29
Lohit & Anjaw	11,402	1,978	3,981	1,642	7,601	66.66	-24	12
Papum Pare	3,462	966	1,509	716	3,191	92.17	-20	3
Tawang	2,172	341	448	388	1,177	54.19	-19	28
Tirap	2,362	714	700	521	1,935	81.92	-17	77
Upper Siang	6,590	1,564	2,452	1,353	5,369	81.47	0	17
Upper Subansiri	7,032	1,800	2,624	1,147	5,571	79.22	16	26
West Siang	8,325	2,656	2,949	1,751	7,356	88.36	49	3
Grand Total	**83,743**	**20,721**	**30,955**	**15,288**	**66,964**	**79.96**	**-190**	**247**

Note: Data of rest districts are not available.

TYPES OF FORESTS

1. **Tropical Forests:** These forests occur up to an elevation of 900 metres above MSL. They are persent in all the districts along the foothills. These forests can further be classified into two main types viz. tropical evergreen forests and tropical semi evergreen forests.

2. **Subtropical Forests:** This type of forests occur in districts between altitudes 800 m to 1900 m. These are essentially evergreen and dense in nature. The trees attain large dimensions (25-40 m high). The forests are rich in species diversity and dominated by Fagaceae members. Luxurious growth of climbers, orchids & ferns, occurs in these forests.

3. **Pine Forests:** These forests extend both in the subtropical and temperate belt in between 1000 m to 1800 m elevation. These are generally met with in rain shadow area and are represented by three different species viz. *Pinus roxburghii, Pinus wallichiana* and *Pinus merkusii.*

4. **Temperate Forests:** Occur in all district as a continuous belt and can be divided into two subtypes viz. Temperate broad leaved forests and Temperate conifer forests.

5. **Alpine Forests:** This type of vegetation occurs on the peaks of higher hills above an altitude of 4000 m upto 5500 m above timber line. For major part of the year, the area is covered by snow and plant activity is restricted to a few months when snow melts.

   As a rule there are no tall trees but dwarf branches and shrubs and mainly herbs with deep roots and cushioned leaves and branches. The profusion of bright coloured flowers which is purely seasonal for a brief period makes the area highly attractive.

6. **Bamboo Forests:** These are seen as bamboo breakes up to 2000 m altitude throughout the State. Bamboos grow mostly in pure stands with very less of associated species. Normally bamboos appear in areas abandoned after shifting cultivation, where they colonise fast. Bamboos of Arunachal Pradesh are *Bambusa tulda, Bambusa pallida, Dendrocalamus hamiltonii, Dendrocalamus hookerii, Pseudostachyum polymorphum, Chimonobambusa* sp., *Cephalostachyum sp. and Arundinaria spp., Phyllostachys sp.* (both single stem bamboos) occur in higher elevation 1000-2000 m.

NATIONAL PARKS & WILDLIFE SANCTUARIES

There are two national parks and eleven wildlife sanctuaries in the State managed by the forest department.

National Parks

S. No.	Name	District	Area in Sq. Kms.	Major animals
1.	Namdhapa National Park (Tiger Project)	Tirap	1985.23	Elephant, Tiger, Gaur, Sambar, Barking Deer, Binturong, Leopard, four Hornbill species, Pea-cock-Pheasant, Kalij Pheasant.
2.	Mouling National Park	East Siang	483.00	Elephant, Barking Deer, Tiger, Leopard, Serow, Birds, Orchids.

Wildlife/Orchid Sanctuaries

S. No.	Name	District	Area in Sq. Kms.	Major animals
1.	Itanagar Wildlife Sanctuary	Papum-Pare	140.30	Elephant, Barking Deer, Tiger, Leopard, Serow, Birds, Orchids.
2.	Dr. D. Ering Memorial Wildlife Sanctuary	Upper Siang	190.00	Honger, Hispid Hore, Bengal florican, Raptors, and migratory water birds.
3.	Mehao Wildlife Sanctuary	Dibang Valley	281.50	Hoolock, Gibbon, Tiger, Leopard, Red panda, Elephant, etc.
4.	Kamlang Wildlife Sanctuary	Lohit	783.00	Hoolock, Gibbon, Tiger, Leopard, Capped Langur, Red panda, Takin.
5.	Eagle Nest Wildlife Sanctuary	West Kameng	217.00	Elephant, Tiger, Leopard, Sambar, Serow, Goral, Red panda, Himalayan Black bear.
6.	Kane Wildlife Sanctuary	West Siang	31.00	Elephant, Small Cats, Deer.
7.	Pakhui Wildlife Sanctuary	East Kameng	861.95	Elephant, Tiger, Gaur, Sambar Barking Deer, Binturong, Leopard, four Hornbill species, Pea-cock-Pheasant, Kalij Pheasant.
8.	Sessa Orchid Sanctuary	West Kameng	100.00	Varieties of orchids, Red Panda, Pheasants, Serow, Goral, etc.
9.	Dibang Wildlife Sanctuary	Dibang Valley	190.00	—
10.	Tale Wildlife Sanctuary	Lower Subansiri	337.00	—
11.	Yordi Rabe Supse Wildlife Sanctuary	West Siang	397.00	—

15 | Education

ARUNACHAL PRADESH, one of the "seven sister states" of the North-East of India is a state with a big vision. The state's educational scenario is slowly improving with the plans and projects initiated by the state as well as the central government. There are two universities in the state including one deemed university for higher learning and several recognized professional colleges. The State is a centre for carrying research works on Yak for which the National Research Centre on Yak (ICAR) has been established at Dirang.

A uniform structure of school education viz., the 10+2 system has been adopted by the schools in Arunachal Pradesh. The primary stage consists of classes I-V, the middle stage from classes VI-VIII and the Secondary Stage consists of Classes IX-X. The higher secondary stage consists of classes XI-XII. The State also provides free education to students up to the age of 14 to universalize elementary education in the State. There are several projects run by local NGOs to make people aware of the importance of education in remote areas. The state's average literacy rate according to 2011 census report was 65.40%.

GROWTH OF EDUCATION IN THE STATE

During the beginning of the 20th century, Arunachal had no schools at all. The first school was established in 1918, in Pasighat, and the second in 1922, in Dambuk. Not surprisingly, both locations bordered the more developed State of Asom, and the establishment of schools went hand in hand with the advancement of regular administration. Progress was slow and, at the time of Independence, there were only three schools in the entire State and, only up to the primary level.

Most people in the State were not familiar with the written word until recently; many did not have a script of their own. The exceptions were the Buddhist tribes of the Kameng region and the Lower Lohit Valley.

The monasteries of the former provided religious instruction in the Tibetan language and, the Khamptis brought with them (from present-day Myanmar) the tradition of reading and writing in the Tai-Khampti language. As a result and out of necessity, knowledge was passed on from generation to generation, through oral histories and learning by doing, and the responsibility of teaching and guiding fell on the older people. The ballads that people sing even today are not just expressions of music and creativity, but, are rooted in time, place, and culture, and have a context. They are an important means of transmitting knowledge.

There were community institutions where young men and women were initiated into their responsibilities and taught skills that were relevant to their needs. In these societies, there was a consequential premium on recall, on precedent and oratory, and on age and experience. The knowledge of farming, of hunting, of conservation, of herbs and medicinal plants, were all passed down from one generation to the next. Social skills and community responsibilities were learnt in the kebangs and community houses.

Newer systems of learning and knowledge have come to Arunachal Pradesh and the domain of knowledge that a person needs to encompass has broadened. The old systems, based on clan and community, have come under stress and have weakened but, they are still very important.

In the 1950s, the old insularity of the State began to come to an end as administrative structures and institutions, akin to that of the rest of the country, were introduced. New towns and settlements began to spring up across the State. In 1951 itself, as many as 67 Lower Primary (LP) schools were set up in the State. From 67 LP schools and one middle school (ME) in 1951-52, the number of schools increased to 179 LP schools, 25 ME schools and seven high schools (HE) in little over a decade.

There were 120 teachers in the LP schools and 6 teachers in the ME schools. To begin with, the enrolment was small. There were 2,674 children in the LP schools and, only 34 children in the ME schools, but, this number grew extremely rapidly as the number of schools expanded.

Number of Schools

Year	Junior Basic Nursery Schools	Pre-Primary/ Upper Primary Schools	Middle/Senior Basic Schools	Secondary/ Higher Secondary Schools
1981	965	–	120	48
1991	–	1,371	254	114
2001	–	1,360	333	184

As above Table shows, there has been a substantial increase in the number of schools and in school enrolment after Arunachal became a State in 1987. The big spurt in the expansion of schools (in all the three categories) was in the 1981-91 period, after which the growth has been more gradual. Between the years 1991 and 2001, the enrolment in middle and secondary schools doubled, and, in the primary schools, it went up by a little over 50 per cent. In terms of number of institutions, the pre-primary/primary schools declined from 1,371 to 1,360 during the years 1991-2001, mainly because of the upgradation of many primary schools to middle schools.

LITERACY

Given the fact that most languages in the region do not have a script of their own, it is not surprising that the literacy levels in the State were extremely low. However, for a people who have recently been introduced to the written word, the progress in the last few decades has been remarkable.

Along with formal education, the literacy rate in Arunachal has also increased considerably. As late as 1981, the literacy rate in Arunachal Pradesh was 25.55 per cent, which means that only one in four people was literate. The literacy rate for men was 35.12 per cent (one in three men was literate) while for women it was only 14.02 per cent (one in seven women was literate). All these rates were substantially below the National average. The literacy rate varied from a high of 34.94 per cent in Lohit district to as low as 9.39 per cent in East Kameng and 15.75 per cent in the Upper Subansiri district. In these two districts (East Kameng and Upper Subansiri) the female literacy rates were as low as 3.52 & 6.48 per cent respectively. The districts of West Kameng, West Siang, East Siang, Dibang Valley, and Lohit enjoyed literacy rates above the State average but, everywhere the literacy levels were low.

Starting from this low literacy rate, the State has made rapid progress. The literacy rate in the State increased from 25.55 per cent in 1981 to 41.59 per cent in 1991 and further to 54.34 per cent in 2001 and 65.40 in 2011. In the 1981-91 decade, the literacy rate for men went up to 51.45 per cent (an increase of 16.33 percentage points). During the same period, the male literacy rate in the country increased by 7.75 percentage points. Not surprisingly, the four districts with the highest literacy rates in 1981, continued to have literacy levels above the State average. West Siang, East Siang, Dibang Valley, Lohit, as well as West Kameng and Changlang had literacy rates above the State average. Tawang, East Kameng, Lower Subansiri, Upper Subansiri, and Tirap continued to have literacy rates below the State average.

Women's literacy rate registered an increase of 15.67 percentage points in the same period. At the national level, the increase in women's literacy rate was 9.53 percentage points in the 1981-91 period. However, women's literacy continued to be low, with a rate of 29.69 per cent, only one in three women in Arunachal was literate. For India as a whole, the literacy rate for women in 1991 was 39.29 per cent. Women's literacy was extremely low in Tawang, East Kameng, and Tirap (all below 20 per cent).

By 2011, the literacy rate in Arunachal Pradesh climbed to 72.60 per cent for men, 57.70 per cent for women and 65.40 per cent for the entire population. Arunachal is ranked at number 34 amongst the 36 States and Union Territories of the country in terms of literacy, according to the 2011 Census. The literacy rate in Arunachal Pradesh is only 7.6 percentage points below the all-India literacy rate of 73.0 per cent. The gap between the literacy rate for India and the State is now 8.3 percentage points for men, 6.9 percentage points for women and 7.6 percentage points for the total population.

Literacy Rates by Sex of State and Districts (2011)

S.No.	State/Districts	Literacy rate*		
		Persons	Male	Female
	Arunachal Pradesh	**65.40**	**72.60**	**57.70**
1.	Tawang	59	67.5	46.5
2.	West Kameng	67.1	73.4	59.1
3.	East Kameng	60	68.6	51.7
4.	Papumpare	80	86.1	73.7
5.	Upper Subansiri	63.8	70	57.6
6.	West Siang	66.5	72.8	59.6
7.	East Siang	72.5	78.5	66.5
8.	Upper Siang	60	66.5	52.6
9.	Changlang	59.8	68.9	49.8
10.	Tirap	52.2	61.9	41.9
11.	Lower Subansiri	74.3	80.5	68.1
12.	Kurung Kumey	48.8	55.1	42.6
13.	Dibang Valley	64.1	68.1	59.2
14.	Lower Dibang Valley	69.1	75.5	62.2
15.	Lohit	68.2	75.5	60
16.	Anjaw	56.5	66.8	43.7

* Literacy rate is the percentage of literates to population aged 7 years and above

GENDER GAP IN LITERACY

Across all the districts and the State, the gender gap in literacy is apparent. As late as the year 2011, there is a difference of more than 14 percentage points between male and female literacy rates. Seven districts (West Kameng, Papum Pare, Lower Subansiri, West Siang, East Siang, Lower Dibang Valley, and

Lohit) have higher literacy rates for women than the State average. However, in Kurung Kumey district, only one out of six women is literate (female literacy is at 17.45 per cent). Women's literacy in Tawang, East Kameng, Kurung Kumey, Lower Subansiri, Upper Subansiri, Upper Siang, Dibang Valley (New), Changlang, and Tirap are all below the State average (43.53 per cent).

Notwithstanding the low literacy rates for women in many parts of the State, rapid gains have been made in women's literacy, and the difference in the literacy rates between men and women in Arunachal is smaller than that in the rest of the country. Following Table shows that the gender gap in Arunachal Pradesh is less than that at the national level, and also shows that the gains in literacy are higher for women than for men, both in Arunachal, and in India, as a whole.

Gender Gap In Literacy

	Literacy Rate-2001		Gender Gap in Literacy	Literacy Rate-2011		Gender Gap in Literacy	Decadal Improvement in Literacy Rate (2001-2011)	
	Males	Females		Males	Females		Males	Females
India	75.20	53.70	21.50	80.9	64.6	16.3	5.7	10.9
Arunachal Pradesh	63.83	43.53	20.30	72.6	57.9	14.7	8.77	14.37

Source: Census of India, 2011.

URBAN-RURAL GAP IN THE LITERACY RATE

As in the rest of India, there is a wide gap between the urban-rural literacy rates in Arunachal too. In 1981, only five districts, West Kameng, Lower Subansiri, West Siang, East Siang, and Lohit had any urban population. The urban-rural gap in the literacy rate for men was 38.30 percentage points, for women the gap was 40.05 percentage points, and for the entire population it was 40.94 percentage points. The urban-rural gap in women's literacy is a little higher than that for men. Of these five districts, with minimal urban area in 1981, the gap was most noticeable in Lower Subansiri and East Siang, although everywhere the urban- rural literacy gaps were high.

By 1991, the urban-rural gap in literacy fell to 30.99 points for men, 36.92 points for women, and 34.57 points for the entire population. The reduction was greater for men (7.31 percentage points) than for women (3.13 percentage points). For the entire population, the urban-rural gap in the literacy rate continued to be quite high, 34.57 per cent (a fall of 6.37 percentage points during 1981-1991). The highest urban -rural gaps in men's literacy were observed in districts like Tirap, West Kameng, Lower Subansiri, and West Siang. Similarly, in women's literacy too, the urban-rural gap was highest in these districts. The smallest gap was observed in East Siang, where, in fact, the gains in literacy seem to be greater in the rural areas than in the urban areas.

An analysis of the urban-rural gap in literacy shows that while the gap is closing, it is as much as 23.0 per cent in 2011, which is of concern. The district-wise data for the year 2011 shows that the gap continues to be particularly large in the districts of Tawang, West Siang, East Kameng, Tirap, and Changlang.

The literacy rate data over the 1981-2011 period shows that the urban-rural gap continues to be large, reinforcing the view that India's development is concentrated in the urban areas. What is of even greater concern is the fact that the urban-rural gap for women is closing slower than that for men. This reflects the fact that education opportunities for women and the girl child in the rural areas continue to be limited.

Urban-Rural Gap In Literacy, Census-2011

District	Urban Literacy Rate (%)	Rural Literacy Rate (%)	Urban-rural Gap (In Percentage Points)
Tawang	90.9	49.1	41.8
West Kameng	78.2	64.4	13.8
East Kameng	77.1	54.8	22.3
Papum-Pare	84.7	73.9	10.8
Upper Subansiri	79.5	60.7	18.8
West Siang	85.4	60.9	24.5
East Siang	80.1	69.6	10.5
Upper Siang	79.2	55.6	23.6
Changlang	84.9	55.8	29.1
Tirap	80.8	45.1	35.7
Lower Subansiri	85.5	72.3	13.2
Kurung Kumey	69.4	48.2	21.2
Dibang Valley	84	55.6	28.4
Lower Dibang Valley	88.4	63.6	24.8
Lohit	80.8	64.4	16.4
Anjaw	80.3	55.2	25.1
Arunachal Pradesh	**82.90**	**59.90**	**23.0**

Urban-rural gap in literacy rates in Arunachal, 1981-2011

1981 1991 2001 2011

- Urban-rural gap in male literacy rate (% age points)   38.30 30.99 27.5 21.0
- Urban-rural gap in female literacy rate (% age points) 40.05 36.92 32.6 24.7
- Urban-rural gap in total literacy rate (% age points)   41.94 34.57 30.5 23.0

HIGHER EDUCATION

The first college for undergraduate study in Arunachal was started in 1964, at Pasighat. Now there are seven Government colleges. They are at Pasighat, Itanagar, Bomdila, Tezu, Along, Khonsa and Changlang. Three new colleges have started at Itanagar, Pasighat and Ziro, with private initiative. There are two universities in the state including one deemed university for higher learning and several recognized professional colleges. Arunachal University (now Rajiv Gandhi University) was established in 1984, with three departments; History, Political Science and Education. Today, it has 14 departments: History, Political Science, Education, English, Tribal Studies, Economics, Botany, Zoology, Geography, Commerce, Hindi, Computer Sciences, Management, and Mathematics. The North Eastern Regional Institute of Science and Technology (NERIST) (Deemed University) was also started in 1984 to provide technical education to the people of North-East India. Some students from Arunachal are enrolled in NERIST. A polytechnic was set up in 2003 with financial assistance from the World Bank. There are two Industrial Training Institutes, one Gramsevak Training Centre, one Auxiliary Nurse Cum-Mid-Wife Training Centre and one College of Horticulture and Forestry, which is under the Central Agricultural University, Manipur.

Educational Institutions In Arunachal Pradesh

S.No.	Item	Unit	As on	
			31.03.2007	**31.03.2008**
1.	University	Nos.	1	1
2.	Engineering Institute (NERIST)	Nos.	1	1
3.	College	Nos.	16	19
4.	Polytechnic	Nos.	1	1
5.	Higher Secondary	Nos.	97	109
6.	Secondary	Nos.	163	171

7.	Middle School	Nos.	664	813
8.	Primary School	Nos.	1561	1721
9.	Total Teaching Staff (School/College/University)	Nos.	14421	14989
10.	Total Students (School/College/University)	'000 Nos.	383	409
11.	Total Schedule Tribe Students (School/College/University)	'000 Nos.	288	308
12.	School for Handicapped	Nos.	1	1
13.	Sport Academy	Nos.	1	1

Source: Arunachal Pradesh at a glance 2009.

NEW DEVELOPMENT

The Rajiv Gandhi University has been converted into a Central University by an Act of Parliament of 9th April 2007. The State Government also took over the Rajiv Gandhi Polytechnic in 2007. One new government College was also established in Yachuli. Similarly, the Arunachal Pradesh State Council of Technical Education was established in June 2007. The State Government has decided to launch the EDUSAT programme with the hub at Rajiv Gandhi University with 50 nos of terminals located at various DIETs and Schools.

16 | Dances and Music

Dance forms an important aspect of the socio-cultural heritage of the people. The dances of the people of Arunachal are group dances—where both men and women take part. There are, however, some dances such as Igu dance of the Mishmi priests, War dances of the Adis, Noctes and Wanchos, Ritualistic dance of the Buddhist tribes, which are male dances. Females are not allowed to dance in these dances.

Some of the popular folk dances of the people are Aji Lamu (Monpa Tribe), Roppi (Nishing Tribe), Hiirii Khaniing (Apatani Tribe), Popir (Adi Tribe), Pasi Kongki (Adi), Chalo (Nocte Tribe), Ponung (Adi Tribe), Rekham Pada (Nishing Tribe), Lion and Peacock dance (Monpa) and so on. Most of the dances are accompanied by songs sung generally in chorus. Musical instruments like drums and Cymbals are played.

The dances, performed by the tribes of Arunachal Pradesh, have been broadly divided into four groups. The first group is the Ritual dances which may again be divided into five sub-groups.

The first sub-groups includes those dances which form part of the various rituals performed to secure prosperity, good health and happiness of the dancer, his family, village or the whole community. The second sub-group comprises of those dances performed in ceremonies related to agriculture and domestication of animals to secure a good harvest and increase of domestic animals respectively. The third sub-group is associated with the funeral ceremony when the soul is guided by a priest to its abode in the land of the dead and to prevent it from haunting its old residence. It is generally believed that if the soul returns to its old home the bereaved family suffers diseases and deaths. The fourth sub-group consists of the fertility dances. These are magical in the sense that the imitation of the movements of coition is believed to promote fertility. War-dances make the fifth sub-group, which are on the decline with the stoppage of internecine feuds and raids. In the old days, when an expeditionary party was successful in killing an enemy or more, the victors used to perform a ceremony on return, so that the spirit of the slain could do no harm to the slayer. Only among the Idu Mishmis, the victim's family also used to perform rites praying for success in taking vengeance. Dance formed a part of this ceremony. The war-dance used to be prevalent among almost all the non-Buddhist tribes.

The second group is the festive-dance which forms the recreational part of a particular festival. The third group is the recreational dances which do not form part of any particular festival or ritual. These are performed on occasions which inspire its participants to express their mirth through these dances. The fourth group is the pantomimes and dance-dramas which narrate a mythical story or illustrate a moral.

SOME IMPORTANT DANCES

Idu Mishmi

Idu Mishmis have a ritual-dance and a fertility-dance. The ritual-dance is performed by the priest or priestess in the ceremonies of Ai-ah, Ai-him, Mesalah and Rren. The fertility-dance is performed on the last day of the Rren ceremony. There is no definite myth about the origin of this ritual dance. According to local tradition, the first priest who officiated in a funeral ceremony was Chineuhu and his brother Ahihiuh, was the first priest who officiated in the other three ceremonies in which this dance forms a part. This dance is associated with the priestly office.

Besides the priest, there are three or four other dancers who are selected from amongst the spectators. In addition it is the usual dress which consists of a loin-cloth, a short-sleeved coat, and a sword slung on the right side, a leather bag slung on the left side and a few bead-necklaces, the priest wears a few other articles. These articles are an apron with particular designs, a head-band decorated with two or three rows of cowries, a necklace studded with the teeth of tiger and bear and a few metal bells. A priestess wears these special articles in addition to the usual Mishmi woman's dress of a skirt, a long sleeved coat and bead-necklaces. The priestess is generally accompanied by female dancers. The accompanying dancers wear the usual dress.

The dancers stand in a line, the priest is second either from the right or left. During the dance, one dancer standing at one end of the line plays a small drum slung from his neck. The priest and the other two dancers play a very small semi-globular single-membrane drum, striking it with a bamboo-stick which is kept tied to the drum with a string. The fifth dancer, if any, plays a horn bugle. When there are five dancers, the priest stands in the middle of the line. He sings a line of invocatory song while all the others play the musical instruments, flex the knees bobbing up and down and alternately raise the right and left heels and stamp these on the ground in time to the drum-beats. When the priest finishes singing the line, others repeat it in chorus. Again the priest sings another line of the song which the others repeat in chorus and thus it goes on.

The priest does not demand any money for his priestly services, but the performer usually remunerates him according to his ability. The remuneration may also be paid in kind, e.g. with handloom coat, brass utensils or pigs.

Digaru Mishmi Buiya Dance

The Digaru Mishmis have two types of dances called Buiya and Nuiya. The Buiya dance has two types of movements and it is performed for entertainment while the Nuiya is a ritual-dance performed by a priest. Buiya dance is performed on any festive occasion like the Duiya, Tazampu and Tanuya festivals which are performed for the prosperity and good health of the performer and his household. This dance may also performed after a feast arranged by a family to entertain the fellow villagers who co-operate with it opening a new field.

The dance is performed in the passage which runs along one side of the house from the front to the rear. Men and women take part in this dance. There is no limit to the age of the dancers although generally children and old persons do not take active part in the dance itself but merely sit by, as spectators. There is no special costume for this dance, so they perform this dance wearing their usual dress. The male dancer wears a loin-cloth a sleeveless jacket, a turban and ear-rings. The female dancer wears a blouse, a long skirt reaching down to the ankle with a short one wrapped over it and a side-bag on the left side. They wear necklaces, large silver-ear-plugs and a silver fillet with its strap studded with coins or cowries.

The dancers stand in a line, one behind the other, in the passage. One of the dancers plays a drum while another plays a gong. Cymbals are played, if available, by another dancer.

Khampti Dance

The Khamptis, who are Buddhists, have many dance-dramas through which they unfold some stories or depict mythical events bearing ethical lessons. These dramas are generally staged during the religious festivals of Potwah, Sankian or Khamsang, constituting the entertainment part of the festivals.

The dance is called 'ka' and the dance-drama is called 'kapung' (ka-dance; pung-story) and actually means a story depicted through the dance. Women do not take part in the drama. The female role, if any, is played by a man in woman's costume.

Ka Fifai Dance-Drama

The Ka Fifai drama is woven round the theme of the traditional belief that ghosts appear and kidnap girls or men and trouble them. The drama opens with a man and his daughter walking in the garden. The ghost appears and captures the girl, and immediately the man greatly aggrieved rushes to the king's court to inform him of the incident and beseech him the rescue his daughter. The king's anger is aroused at this news and he calls for his Ministers and asks them to prepare for war. The King's men go in search of the ghost and bring him before the king, who severely warns him never to do such a thing again. The ghost frightened bows before the king and with this ends the drama.

Ponung Dance (Adis)

Adi village has a rich cultural life. The tribal people are famous for their Ponung that is dancing with the accompaniment of songs. A group of girls dance in a circle holding each other by stretching their hands over each others shoulders while the leader-usually a man called the Miri-dances and sings in the centre-holding aloft and shaking a sword like musical instrument called 'Yoksha'. First he sings a line and then it is repeated in chorus by the maidens rhythmically in circle at a low pace. On all important occasions ponung is arranged.

Sadinuktso (Akas)

The Akas have a number of dances and songs for the different socio-religious festivities. One of the well known dance among the Akas is the Sadinuktso. A member from the boy's group comes forward, gives his performance for a short while and recedes. A girl then comes and she also dances all alone. This relation goes on till all the boys and girls of the group have danced. No song is sung with this dance. It is generally performed in marriages, guest, entertainments or on the construction of a new house.

Mask-Dance

Religious belief of some tribal communities especially in Arunachal Pradesh have been influenced in some respect by Hinduism and Buddhism. The Sherdukpens and the Monpas perform many kind of ritual masked dances of which Thutotdam is most fascinating. The dancers put on masks representing skulls and wear costumes designed as skeletons. The ritualistic dance depicts how the soul after death is received in the other world. At Torgyap Festival many such kinds of masked dances are performed which aim at driving away evil spirits and ensuring prosperity, good harvest and favourable weather throughout the year.

The Monpas perform Arpos dance in which about twenty-five dancers, wearing helmets and carrying sword and shields like ancient warrior, depicts how the ancestors of the tribe conquered their enemies. The performance concludes with a dance number called Gallong Chham in which about ten dancers perform wearing very colourful costumes and sumptuous headgear.

Of all the masked pantomimes that the Sherdukpens perform, the most fascinating is the Yak dance. The dummy animal is formed by two men concealed behind a black cloth that forms its body. The head of the dummy Yak is made of wood. On its back sits the figure of a goddess. Three masked men dance around the dummy animal.

Folk Dances of Arunachal Pradesh

S.No.	Name of the Tribes	Name of Dances
1.	Adi	Ponung, Taapu, Yakjong etc.
2.	Adi-Galo	Ami Henam, Tanu, Popir, Eme-relo, Boi-take, etc.
3.	Aka	Niechu dou, Dogoh dou
4.	Apatani	Paktu-Itu, Demindu etc.
5.	Hill Miri	Boyen or Kuba Tondore, Pojuh, Nitin, Ponung
6.	Khamti	Kakong Tokai, Kachang Aluwang, Ka-Fifai dance drama, Ka-Mukcho
7.	Khamba	Troh, Guru Chanji Pantomime, Padi or Sethoh Pantomime
8.	Khowa	Gasisiu, Clown etc.
9.	Miji	Dumai, Jei etc.
10.	Mishmi	Idu, Ah-ih, Mesala, Nuiyaidu, Digaru-Beeiya, Nuiya

S.No.	Name of the Tribes	Name of Dances
11.	Memba	Broh dance, Bardo pantomime
12.	Monpa	Yak, Lion & Peacock, Deer pantomime, Ajjlamu pantomime, Broh and other monastic dances
13	Nishing	Rikhampada, Buiya, Juju-Jaja etc.
14	Nocte	Laku Bawang, Mang Buang, Ramvan Boung etc.
15.	Singpho	Manglup ceremony and dance
16.	Sherdukpen	Jam or Bardo, Yak pantomime, Jik Charm or Seeh pantomime, Brohpu etc.
17.	Tagin	Si-Ome, Nibutamu dance etc.
18.	Thangsa	Moh festival dance, Sapoloso dance etc.

MUSIC

Following are the chief folk songs of Arunachal, sung on different festivals and occasion :

Ja-Jin-Ja

On occasion of feasts and merriment, during marriages or other social meets, this song is sung. Both men and women sing it in chorus or individually. But once the song starts, all those who are present join them in singing.

Baryi

It is a song which narrate their history, their religious lore and mythology. Its whole cycle takes hours to complete. It is also a feature of festivals or of occasion of important social or religious gatherings.

Nyioga

It is sung when a marriage ceremony is concluded and the bridal party returns leaving the bride in her home. The theme is that of the joy. It contains pieces of advice to the bride for her future life.

17 | Art and Crafts

ARUNACHAL PRADESH is the home to a large number of tribes and sub-tribes. It has a rich tradition of craftsmenship, which manifests itself in various arts and crafts produced by these tribes. The Buddhist including Monpas, Sherdukpen, Aka make beautiful masks, carpets and painted wooden vessels. The Bangis and Apatani make bag, hat, jewellery etc. Khamtis and Wanchos are well known for their wood carving. Pottery of Nyishi women is well-known. From the point of view of art and culture the area may very conveniently be divided into three zones.

The first zone includes the Buddhist tribes i.e., the Sherdukpens and Monpas and also to some extent the Khowa, Aka and Miji group. The people of the first one make beautiful masks. They also periodically stage pantomimes and mask dances. Making of beautiful carpets, painted wooden vessels and silver articles are, however, the speciality of the Monpas.

The people of the second zone are expert workers in cane and bamboo. The Apatanis, Hill Miris and Adis make beautiful articles of these materials, which speak eloquently about their skill in handicrafts. The second cultural zone occupies the central part from East Kameng in the west to Lohit in the east. The third zone is formed by the south-eastern part of the territory. They also weave articles that are in common use in their daily life.

The people of the third zone are famous for their woodcarving. The Wanchos, however, weave beautiful bag and loin-cloth also. Goat's hair, ivory, boar's tusks, beads of agates and other stones as well as of brass and glass are special fascinations of the people of this zone.

WOOD-CARVING

The Monpas, Khamtis, and Wanchos occupy significant place in this art. The Monpa wood carver make beautiful cups, dishes, fruit bowls and carve magnificent masks for ceremonial dances and pantomimes. Wooden masks are also carved by the Khambas and Membas of West Siang. The Khamptis make beautiful religious images, figures of dancers, toys and other objects. Very beautiful wood carvings are made by the Wanchos of Tirap.

In fact the Wancho area is the Chief centre of wood carving. Wancho wood carving was earlier associated mainly with head hunting and human head dominated everything that they made. But nowadays variety of subjects are included. They are invariably free standing. Minute observation on the details will reveal that the Wancho wood carver had deep sense of proportion, inspite of the fact that they give much attention to the head.

Of late departure from the traditional fixed form is noticed in many carved figures. Symmetrical postures are replaced by assymetrical ones, relief works are experimented in various themes. There is no doubt that change has penetrated deep into the Wancho wood-carving.

CANE AND BAMBOO WORK

Cane and bamboo industry of Arunachal Pradesh is of very high standard. Most of the domestic requirements are made of cane and bamboo. Hats of different sizes and shapes, various kinds of baskets, cane vessels, a wide variety of cane belts, woven and plains, elaborately woven brassier of cane and fibre, bamboo mugs with carvings, a variety of ornaments and necklace are some of the products that deserve special mention. The technique of basketry is same throughout. The two basic techniques are twill and hexagon both open and closed.

Arunachal basketery are beautiful not only because of the fine texture but also because of the unusual shapes. Many a baskets have pleasing forms. There is definite correlation between the shape and the topography and climatic condition of the region.

SMOKING PIPES

Palibos are fond of smoking therefore make smoking pipes from wood and bamboo roots, but they also procure metallic pipes through barter trade from their neighbours the Bokars, the Ramos and the Membas.

1. **Elak-Tidu:** Smoking pipe made of wood.
2. **Ete-Tidu:** Smoking pipe made of bamboo-root.
3. **Ra-Tidu:** Metallic pipe engraved and with a long neck.
4. **Ata-Tidu:** Smoking pipe made of silver.

CARPET MAKING

Carpet making is the speciality of the Monpas. They weave lovely colourful carpets with dragon, geometric and floral designs. The choice of colour and the colour combination is unique. Though originally they weave carpet for domestic use, it has now become an item of trade and a major occupation for some ladies.

ORNAMENTS

Ornament making is another craft widely practised in Arunachal Pradesh. Besides beads of various colours and sizes blue feathered wings of birds and green wings of beetles are also used in decoration. The Akas make bamboo bangles and ear ornament which are sometimes decorated with pucker work designs.

Most of the ornaments are made of beads as the tribes are very fond of it. While some people just hang strings of beads round their neck, others such as the Noctes and Wanchos weave them into very attractive patterns. The Wancho girls particularly are very expert in bead work. The designs and colour combination are superb. Besides beads work the Wanchos make ear ornaments from glass beads, wild seeds, cane, bamboo and reed. Various ornaments of coloured glass beads hold a special fascination for the people of Arunachal Pradesh.

Silver ornaments are a speciality of the Mishmis. The Idu Mishmi women wear silver fillet necklaces with lockets and beautiful earring. The Sherdukpens and the Khamtis at one time were also renowned for silver work. The Apatani women wear nose plugs made of cane which are an exception with the other people of the territory.

The gallong women wear ear-plugs and the earring. Plugs are generally of leaf, wood or bamboo, while the rings are heavy for they are made of iron. The rings are coiled in several turns and specially used by the Karka Gallong women. Very often women have their ear-lobes slashed due to the heavy weight of the ornaments.

WEAPONS

Weapons are an integral part of the tribal life since the times immemorial. Although certain weapons have become obsolete and replaced by modern weapons yet traditional weapons have a place of their own. Weapons are used in war and chase and day to day task. All such weapons are produced locally. The most important weapon of Akas is bow and arrow, known by the names of tkeri and moo respectively, and used extensively in the chase. Weapons may vary in size according to the user`s requirement. The bigger ones used in hunting are fitted with tips of iron and smeared with poison. The bows are usually hung over the shoulders while the arrows are carried in a case of bamboo called Thouvou.

Another weapon, originally of war but now of defence, is a kind of crude harpoon, one end of which is barbed with sharp iron nails. It is hurled at the target from a distance. The most common weapon used both in war and peace is the dao. It is of extensive use to the people in their day-to-day task such as cutting wood and bamboo pieces, clearing shrubs and other growth in the forest etc. It is made of steel and is usually covered with bamboo sheath when not in use. The local term for dao is wetz.

Like Akas, Pailibos also use different kinds of weapon. They keep it in a special place. Some of the weapons used by them are as follows-

1. UYI—A bamboo bow with a cane string.
2. UPUK—A bamboo arrow without an iron tip or a poison.
3. MORA—A bamboo arrow with an iron tip.
4. GEB-BU—A quiver made from hollow bamboo with a bamboo lid.
5. NYIBU—A pointed spear with long wooden pole and iron blade. It has a shaft made of a long pole of dry and hard wood. Below the metal head there is tuft of yak or horse hair.
6. YOKSE—A big steel dao or sword.
7. SOTAM—A shield made of bamboo and cane.
8. CHOBUK—It is a sheath for the dao or medium size dagger made from cane and strengthened with pieces of wooden strips.
9. EG-GYI—An iron axe used for felling trees and for slaughtering mithuns during sacrifice.

POTTERY

Nyishi women are skilled in this craft. The legend is that Abo Takam was the first Nyishi potter and from him the art passed on to the women. The process involves pounding a specific kind of earth called dekam on a big stone with a wooden hammer. When it turns into powder, water is mixed and it is hammered till it gains the required softness. Clay lumps are taken home. The woman sits with a piece of gunny bag, or old fibre blanket spread over her thigh. She takes a lump and shapes it with her finger into a crude pot with a shallow opening at the top and rim round it. When several such crude pots have been shaped they are kept in the top-most tray over the hearth to dry. Next day they are ready for the final processing. This is done by pushing a stone deeper and deeper through the hollow of the mouth to get the right bulge of the sides, which are beaten on the outer side with a kamgi to flatten them thin. The kamgi is a bamboo stick with a lineal design on it. It leaves the marks of the design on the body of the pot. The process is continued till the desired round shape, size and finish are obtained.

Finished pots are not subjected to any polishing or burnishing. They are carefully kept in the shade while drying. When completely dry, they are put in a fire out-side the house. There are no kilns or pot-ovens, though a ditch, if available, makes it convenient to put burning firewood over the pots. More or less forty minutes are sufficient to bake a pot. Pottery is exclusively limited to cooking utensils.

WEAVING

Weaving is the occupation of the womenfolk throughout, the territory. They are very particular about colours and have a beautiful sense of colour combination. The favourite colours are black, yellow, dark blue, and green. Originally they used natural dye but nowadays they switch over to synthetic dyes available in the market. The designs are basically geometrical type varying from a formal arrangement of lines and bands to elaborate patterns of diamonds and lozenges. These designs are sometimes enhanced by internal repetition and other decorations.

A few of the woven products that deserves mention are Sherdukpen shawls, Apatani jackets and scarves, Adi skirts, jackets and bags, Mishmi shawls, blouses and jackets and Wancho bags and loin cloths. Although fly shuttles are now being introduced particularly in the government run weaving centres, the traditional loin looms are still in use and the genuine textiles are products of these looms.

18 | Fairs and Festivals

FAIRS and festivals form an integral and indigenous part of the life of the native people of Arunachal Pradesh. They seem to show fanaticism towards their religion. Festivals and fairs are a means for the tribal population to exult themselves and pray to the Almighty to bestow upon them good health, perpetual bliss, happiness and wealth. Their glorious heritage with enchanting folk songs, dances and exotic ways of prayers, express their friendly simplicity and modesty. Their fairs and festivals match their faith. Animal sacrifice is a common ritual in most festivals.

The list of festivals in Arunachal Pradesh is a very long one, as each season brings along a new festive season for the people. The "Losar" festival of the Monpas mark the onset of the new year for the tribes. The festival is celebrated for five consecutive days. They dance and offer prayers to welcome the New Year with lots of enthusiasm so that it brings along all that is good and eliminates the bad things from their life. Another festival that is also celebrated for peace and prosperity is the "Reh" festival associated with the "Idu Mishmis." This also lasts for six days.

During the month of March comes the most popular festival of Arunachal called "Ojiyale". This festival also stretches out for twelve long days and the tribals are once again busy with prayers, melodious songs and dances. The Digarus Mishmis perform "Tamladu" festival of earth and water, which is indeed a prayer to the Almighty to protect them against any unseen natural calamities.

Festivals therefore represent a meeting place for the tribals of Arunachal Pradesh to form a jamboree and perform variety of dance, songs, stage pantomime and masked dances. Their lives are incomplete without these offerings and the typical music and dance which imbibes the essence of tribal culture and tradition. Arunachal Pradesh is also the proud host of the

International Angling Festival. The angling festival held in this homeland of 27 distinct and culturally rich tribes, is one of its unique kind in the whole world.

IMPORTANT FESTIVALS OF ARUNACHAL PRADESH

CHOEKHOR

After the crops are sown and at the time of little agricultural activity, in the seventh month of lunar calendar, a rite known as "Choekhor" is organised in the villages by the entire village community with the aim of offering supernatural protection to the crops sown, for good harvest and to drive away evil spirits.

LOSAR

The New Year festival, called "Losar", is perhaps the most important festival of Tawang district. The Losar festival of the Monpas is their new year of festival. On this occasion people clean out their homes to usher in the new year and to discard the old. It mostly falls in the last part of February or early part of March and is celebrated with lots of fun and festivity, which lasts for about 8 to 15 days.

TORGYA

Torgya is a monastic festival held every year for three days starting from 28th day of the eleventh month of the lunar calendar, which generally falls in the last part of January. In order to drive off evil forces and to ward off any natural calamity. Monastic dances are performed for 3 days during Torgya festivals.

JOMU

A religious festivals of the Monpas, this is a get together sort of festival which is observed after the completion of sowing of seeds between the 5th and 6th months of Monpa, Lunar calendar. In this festival the villagers go to the Gompa in their traditional dress. The function is graced by the oldest member of the village.

CHOSKER

In this religious festival of Monpas, the Lamas (Buddhist priests) read religious scriptures in the Gompa (Buddhist temple) for a number of days. Thereafter the villagers carry the religious books on their back in a procession under the guidance of senior Lama. The procession goes round the cultivated fields which fall within the jurisdiction of the village. The significance of this performance is to ensure better cultivation and protect the grains from the insects and wild animals and also for the prosperity of the villagers. Normally this festival is performed during the months of April-May, after the Jhum fields are prepared. The ritual involves the suspension of all outside activities for a definite period.

SAGA DAWA

The 4th month as per lunar calendar is regarded as the holiest period for the Buddhists. This month marks the birth of Lord Buddha, his attainment of supreme enlightenment and his passing into the state of nirvana. It normally falls in the month of May. This occasion is celebrated with much fun and gaiety.

TAMLADU FESTIVAL

Another important festival is Tamladu, essentially celebrated by the Digaru Mishmis tribe. During the festival, prayers are offered to the God of Earth and the God of Water for protection against natural calamities. The supreme-Lord Jebmalu, is worshipped and welfare of human beings, the standing crops and domestic animals.

SANGKEN FESTIVAL

Sangken festival, is an occasion to bathe the images of Lord Buddha ceremoniously. This also heralds the new year and people sprinkle water on each other as a sign of merriment.

KHAN FESTIVAL

Another festival is the Khan festival, an occasion for the reunion of the people. Besides the usual festivities, the significance of the festival lies in the ceremony whereby the priest ties a piece of wool around everybody's neck. The belief is that the enchanted thread will bring good luck to each of them.

19 | Tourism

TAWANG: Tawang, the land of the Monpa and Sherdukpen tribes with centuries-old monastery, Dragon gates, hundred pristine lakes and numerous waterfalls, situated high up in the misty-eyed Eastern Himalaya. The true beauty lies in the unpampered vistas, serenity of its lakes, restlessness of brooks, and the spiritual fragrance and ever smiling people.

The soggy, rocky mountains, snowcapped summits and old Monasteries looming large in the skyline, are the real treasures of the place. The township stands on the spur of a hill over 12,000 ft. above the sea level. It is the major centre of the Mahayana Buddhist and the headquarters of Tawang district.

TAWANG MONASTERY: Tawang is famous for its 400 years old Buddhist Monastery locally called Gumpha. It is India's largest Buddhist Monastary. It is the fountainhead of spiritual life of the followers of the Gellupa sect of the Mahayana school of Buddhism. The Tawang Monastery is associated with the famous Torgva festival which is held in the eleventh Monpa month called the Dawa Chukchipah during Dec.–Jan. as per the Buddhist Calendar. The Tibetan influence here is unmistakable, with the elaborately painted wooden windows and other motifs. Prayer flags flutter in the breeze outside. There is an 8 metre high gilded statue of Lord Buddha here. A must visit is the craft centre which produces very fine woolen carpets of colourful designs and masks.

SE LA PASS: Se La Pass, lies on the way to Tawang. The highest pass of the state of Arunachal Pradesh and the third highest of the world is a wonderful place to visit.

PAKANG TENG TSO LAKE: Pakang Teng Tso Lake, the spectacular lake lies at about 17km from Tawang and a dazzling example of the hidden treasure amidst the vast green vegetation.

TIPI: Tipi, Asia's largest orchidarium, the Orchid Research Centre is located here in the West Kameng district. The Orchid centre on the bank of river Bharali, surrounded by evergreen forest has more than 500 species of orchids. On display are some of the finest species with names like the Dainty Lady's Slipper or the more formal sounding Dendrobium. Arunachal has the largest range of orchids in India and at Tipi; scientists are creating new, hybrid species using the latest techniques of bio-technology.

ITANAGAR: Itafort is a historical fort situated at the heart of the capital complex in Papum Pare District. It is a fort of irregular shape, built mainly with bricks. Total brick work is of 16,200 cubic metres, length. There are three gates on three sides viz; Eastern, Western, and Southern which is said to be built by Ahoms. It is estimated that more than 80 lakhs of bricks, 45 cubic metres of stone and 46,300 mandays were required to build the fort. Besides this, other places of interest are the Buddhist Monastery, Jawaharlal Nehru Memorial Museum, and Emporium and Ganga Lake where boating facilities are available.

ZIRO: A picturesque valley of the Apatani plateau to the north of Itanagar. The valley is surrounded with pine covered mountains. The place is the home of Apatani tribes. High altitude fish farm, Pine Bamboo groves, villages, indigenous method of rice cultivation, craft centre are the major attraction of the place. The smell of the mist, the taste of the breeze and the sound of the forest make it worth travel. The place is an Anthropologist's delight.

DAPORIJO: Daporijo is a large village town situated at the confluence of the Sippi and Subansiri rivers. It is the District Headquarters of Upper Subansiri district and is situated on the right bank of River Subansiri. Places of interest are the local villages in and around and a beautiful cave a few kilometres away. The place is ideal for trekking and angling on River Subansiri.

TEZU: Tezu has the Parasuram Kund where, particularly during winter, a fair is held during Makar-Sankranti. Pilgrims from all over the country come here for a holy dip in the Kund. There is a large lake called Glow Lake, which can be reached by foot.

BOMDILA: The headquarters of West Kameng district is situated at a height of 8,500 ft. Offers spectacular panoramic views of Himalayan landscapes and snow clad mountains. This area has had strong Tibetan and Buddhist influences over many centuries and hence there are many Buddhist monasteries called 'Gompas' here.

There is a craft centre here which produces very fine carpets of colourful designs and masks. Other places of interest here are apple orchards and the Ethnographic Museum. Bomdila also offers a bird's eye view of Kangto and Gorichen peaks (the highest peaks of the state) amidst the Himalayan landscape and snow clad ranges.

DIRANG: Dirang is the sub-divisional headquarters in West Kameng district, situated between Bomdila and Tawang. Places of interest are Apple and Kiwi orchards, National Yak Research and Breeding Centre at Nigmadung, Sheep breeding farm, Sangti Valley (9 kms from Dirang) hot spring few kilometres from Dirang where people go for a holy dip to wash away sins and diseases.

DAPORIJO: Headquarters of Upper Subansiri district and is situated on the right bank of River Subansiri. Places of interest are the local villages in and around and a beautiful cave a few kilometres away. The best season to visit is from October to April.

PASIGHAT: Headquarters of East Siang district, situated on the right bank of river Siang. Siang is the name of river Brahmaputra in Arunachal Pradesh. A visit to Dr. D. Ering Wildlife Sanctuary where wild buffalos, tigers, samber, deer and wild ducks are found in plenty is a must. Other places of interest are the surrounding villages and the Emporium. Pasighat is ideal for river rafting, boating, angling, trekking and hiking. The Brahmaputra Darshan, festival has become a bi-annual fest.

BRAHMKUND: It is near the border towards China and Myanmar where the Brahamputra zooms a lake. It is a pilgrimage centre on Makar Sankranti day in mid-January.

❖ ❖ ❖

20 | Indigenous Games

HOLE TASO DUKANARAM: Hole Taso Dukanaram is a peculiar game which involves the imitation of an animal called Hole Taso. This animal is quite like a cat, and runs around beating its chest alternately with both its front paws. Another remarkable feature of this animal is its ability to hold a third leg in the air, while scampering around. Consequently, the game tests a contestant's overall balance, strength and coordination.

HINAM TURNAM: The local people call it the struggle of life and death. In this game, the participants assume the role of the hunter and the hunted in the forest. The dilemma of the hapless hunter, who having missed the prey due to poor marksmanship, follows and catches up with it and seizes it by the third leg, is also part of the game.

POROK-PAMIN SINAM OR COCK-FIGHTING: With one leg held in his hand and the other hand on his shoulder, the contestant has one leg to hop on, and achieve his objective of pushing his opponent out of the circle. Any of the two players who falls to the ground, or loses his hold on his leg, or steps out of the circle, is disqualified.

MAJONG: It is a game played by four persons with small tiles in which the players pick up and discard tiles until one of them has a winning combination.

ARCHERY: This is one of the most popular games played by male folk of Monpa tribe especially during the period of Losar festival which generally falls in the month of February. The Bow and arrows are made of Bamboo and tagged placed at about 50 to 100 metres distance.

PANGER: It is shot put played by the menfolk.

21 | Appendix

District-wise Rural-Urban Population-2011

State/ District Code	State/District	Population 2011		
		Total	Rural	Urban
1	2	3	4	5
	Arunachal Pradesh	**13,83,727**	**10,66,358**	**3,17,369**
01	Tawang	49,977	38,775	11,202
02	West Kameng	83,947	68,015	15,932
03	East Kameng	78,690	60,340	18,350
04	Papum Pare	1,76,573	79,610	96,963
05	Upper Subansiri	83,448	70,043	13,405
06	West Siang	1,12,274	87,306	24,968
07	East Siang	99,214	71,579	27,635
08	Upper Siang	35,320	28,780	6,540
09	Changlang	1,48,226	1,28,998	19,228
10	Tirap	1,11,975	91,165	20,810
11	Lower Subansiri	83,030	70,224	12,806
12	Kurung Kumey	92,076	89,731	2,345
13	Dibang Valley	8,004	5,620	2,384
14	Lower Dibang Valley	54,080	42,691	11,389
15	Lohit	1,45,726	1,13,296	32,430
16	Anjaw	21,167	20,185	982

Rural-Urban Population-2011 (Figures at a glance)

	Population 2011			Literates (%)		
	Total	Rural	Urban	Total	Rural	Urban
Persons	13,83,727	10,66,358	3,17,369	65.4	59.9	82.9
Males	7,13,912	5,46,011	1,67,901	72.6	67.4	88.4
Females	6,69,815	5,20,347	1,49,468	57.7	52.0	76.7

Rural-Urban Population (0-6)-2011 (Figures at a glance)

	Population (0-6) (Absolute)			Percentage to total Population		
	Total	Rural	Urban	Total	Rural	Urban
Persons	2,12,188	1,72,289	39,899	15.33	16.15	12.57
Males	1,07,624	87,241	20,383	15.07	15.97	12.13
Females	104,564	85,048	19,516	15.61	16.34	13.05

Multiple-Choice Questions

1. Tawang monastery is situated in—
   A. Lohit   B. West Siang   C. East Siang   D. None of these

2. Sixth Dalai Lama Tsangyemg Gyatso was born in—
   A. Tawang   B. Along   C. Anini   D. None of these

3. At present, the total number of districts in Arunachal Pradesh is—
   A. 25   B. 14   C. 13   D. None of these

4. On which year NEFA was upgraded as Union Territory of Arunachal Pradesh?
   A. 1974   B. 1972   C. 1980   D. None of these

5. On which year Arunachal Pradesh became 24th State of the Indian Union?
   A. 1957   B. 1987
   C. 1992   D. None of these

6. Area of the Arunachal Pradesh is—
   A. 80,000 sq.km   B. 83,743 sq.km   C. 87,543 sq.km   D. None of these

7. Arunachal Pradesh comprises _______ of the country's total area.
   A. 2.55%   B. 5.55%   C. 4.25%   D. None of these

8. Name of the capital of Arunachal Pradesh is—
   A. Ziro   B. Itanagar   C. Khonsa   D. None of these

9. Bumla Pass is situated in—
   A. Assam (Asom)   B. Sikkim
   C. Arunachal Pradesh   D. None of these

10. What is the name of the headquarter of West Kameng district?
    A. Bomdila   B. Tawang   C. Seppa   D. None of these

11. Headquarter of East Kameng district is—
    A. Ziro   B. Along   C. Seppa   D. None of these

12. Latitude of Arunachal Pradesh is—
A. 26°28' N to 29°30' N
B. 20°28'N to 21°24' N
C. 35°24' N to 36°24' N
D. None of these

13. Longitude of Arunachal Pradesh is—
A. 90° E to 95° E
B. 85°87' E to 89°90' E
C. 91°30' E to 97°30' E
D. None of these

14. Arunachal Pradesh Mineral Development & Trading Corporation Ltd. was set up in–
A. 1980　　　B. 1991　　　C. 1995　　　D. None of these

15. Main crop of Arunachal Pradesh is—
A. Maize　　　B. Rice　　　C. Wheat　　　D. None of these

16. Deopani Multipurpose Project is located in—
A. Lower Dibang Valley district
B. East Kameng district
C. Lohit district
D. None of these

17. In Arunachal Pradesh total forest area is—
A. 66,964 sq.km　B. 60,562 sq.km　C. 55,432 km　D. None of these

18. Total number of National Parks in Arunachal Pradesh is—
A. Two　　　B. Three　　　C. Four　　　D. None of these

19. Which among the following district has maximum per cent of forest cover?
A. Siang East　　B. Siang West　　C. Papum-Pare　D. None of these

20. Which among the following district has minimum per cent of forest cover?
A. Tirap　　　B. Lohit　　　C. Tawang　　　D. None of these

21. Namdhapa National Park is located in—
A. Tirap
B. Tawang
C. Lohit
D. None of these

22. Mouling National Park is situated in—
A. East Siang district
B. Lohit district
C. Papum-Pare district
D. None of these

23. Largest State of North-East India is—
A. Assam (Asom)
B. Tripura
C. Arunachal Pradesh
D. None of these

24. Population density of Arunachal Pradesh is—
A. 150　　　B. 325　　　C. 15　　　D. 17

25. According to 2011 census, total population of Arunachal Pradesh is—
A. 12,13,437   B. 8,73,241   C. 13,83,727   D. None of these

26. Decadal growth (2001-2011) of population of Arunachal Pradesh is—
A. 20%   B. 26.0%   C. 30%   D. None of these

27. Total literacy rate (2011 census) in Arunachal Pradesh is—
A. 55%   B. 60%   C. 65.40%   D. None of these

28. Male literacy rate in Arunachal Pradesh is—
A. 80.54%   B. 72.60%   C. 75%   D. None of these

29. Female literacy rate in Arunachal Pradesh is—
A. 83.44%   B. 45.53%   C. 57.70%   D. None of these

30. According to the 2011 census, the ST population constitutes......per cent of the total population of Arunachal Pradesh.
A. 80%   B. 68.8%   C. 70%   D. None of these

31. Which district has maximum ST population concentration?
A. Tawang   B. Kurung Kumey C. West Siang   D. None of these

32. Sex ratio in Arunachal Pradesh is—
A. 938   B. 912   C. 1001   D. None of these

33. Longest national highways of Arunachal Pradesh is—
A. NH-52   B. NH-153   C. NH-1   D. None of these

34. Arunachal Pradesh State Transport Services (APSTS) was started in the year—
A. 1975   B. 1980   C. 1970   D. None of these

35. In Arunachal Pradesh, the main source of generation of power is—
A. Diesel   B. Gas   C. Hydel   D. None of these

36. The first college for undergraduate study in Arunachal Pradesh was started in—
A. 1960   B. 1962   C. 1964   D. None of these

37. Rajiv Gandhi University was established in—
A. 1984   B. 1990   C. 1960   D. None of these

38. Rajiv Gandhi University is a—
A. Central University   B. State University
C. Deemed University   D. None of these

39. Arunachal Pradesh Legislative Assembly consists of—
A. 40 members   B. 60 members   C. 50 members D. None of these

40. In Lok Sabha, Arunachal Pradesh has—
A. 1 member   B. 2 members   C. 4 members   D. None of these

41. In Rajya Sabha, Arunachal Pradesh has—
A. 1 member   B. 2 members   C. 3 members   D. None of these

42. Ponung is a dance of—
A. Adi tribes   B. Aptani tribes   C. Khamti   D. None of these

43. Sadinuktso is a famous dance of—
A. Akas tribes   B. Khamba   C. Mishmi   D. None of these

44. Baryi is a famous—
A. Folk dance   B. Folk song   C. Hill-Station   D. None of these

45. Orchid Research Centre is located in—
A. Tipi   B. Itanagar   C. Ziro   D. None of these

46. Parasuram Kund is located in—
A. Tezu   B. Tipi   C. Itanagar   D. None of these

47. National Yak Research and Breeding Centre is situated at—
A. Nigmadung   B. Tezu   C. Tipi   D. None of these

48. Pasighat is situated on—
A. Siang river   B. Tirap river
C. Subansiri river   D. None of these

49. State bird of Arunachal Pradesh is—
A. Hornbill   B. Mithun   C. Parrot   D. None of these

50. State animal of Arunachal Pradesh is—
A. Elephant   B. Yak   C. Mithun   D. None of these

ANSWERS

1	2	3	4	5	6	7	8	9	10
D	A	A	B	B	B	A	B	C	A

11	12	13	14	15	16	17	18	19	20
C	A	C	B	B	A	A	A	C	C

21	22	23	24	25	26	27	28	29	30
D	A	C	D	C	B	C	B	C	B

31	32	33	34	35	36	37	38	39	40
B	A	B	A	C	C	A	A	B	B

41	42	43	44	45	46	47	48	49	50
A	A	A	B	A	A	A	A	A	C

———

1912

www.ingramcontent.com/pod-product-compliance
Lightning Source LLC
LaVergne TN
LVHW050644200726
843506LV00010B/1361